MEDIUM RARE

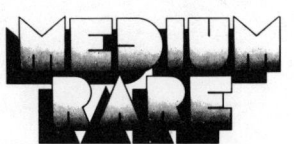

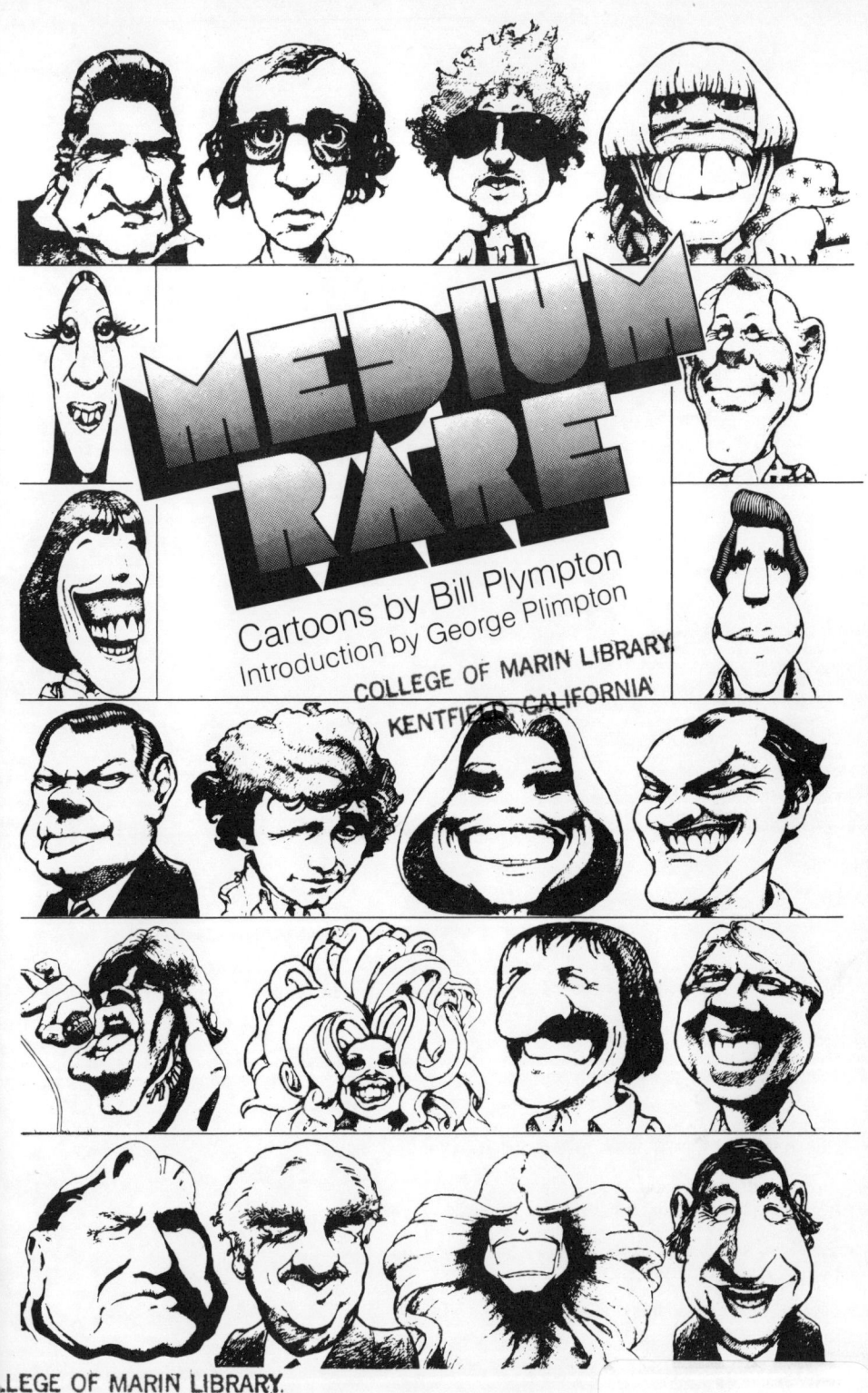

MEDIUM RARE

Cartoons by Bill Plympton

Introduction by George Plimpton

Holt, Rinehart and Winston
New York

Published simultaneously in Canada
by Holt, Rinehart and Winston of Canada, Limited.

Library of Congress Catalog Card Number: 77-15209
ISBN: 0-03-021466-1

First Edition

Printed in the United States of America
10 9 8 7 6 5 4 3 2 1

I want to thank
Michael Goldstein, Dan Georgakas,
Ellen Datlow, and Don Hutter
for helping to make this book possible.

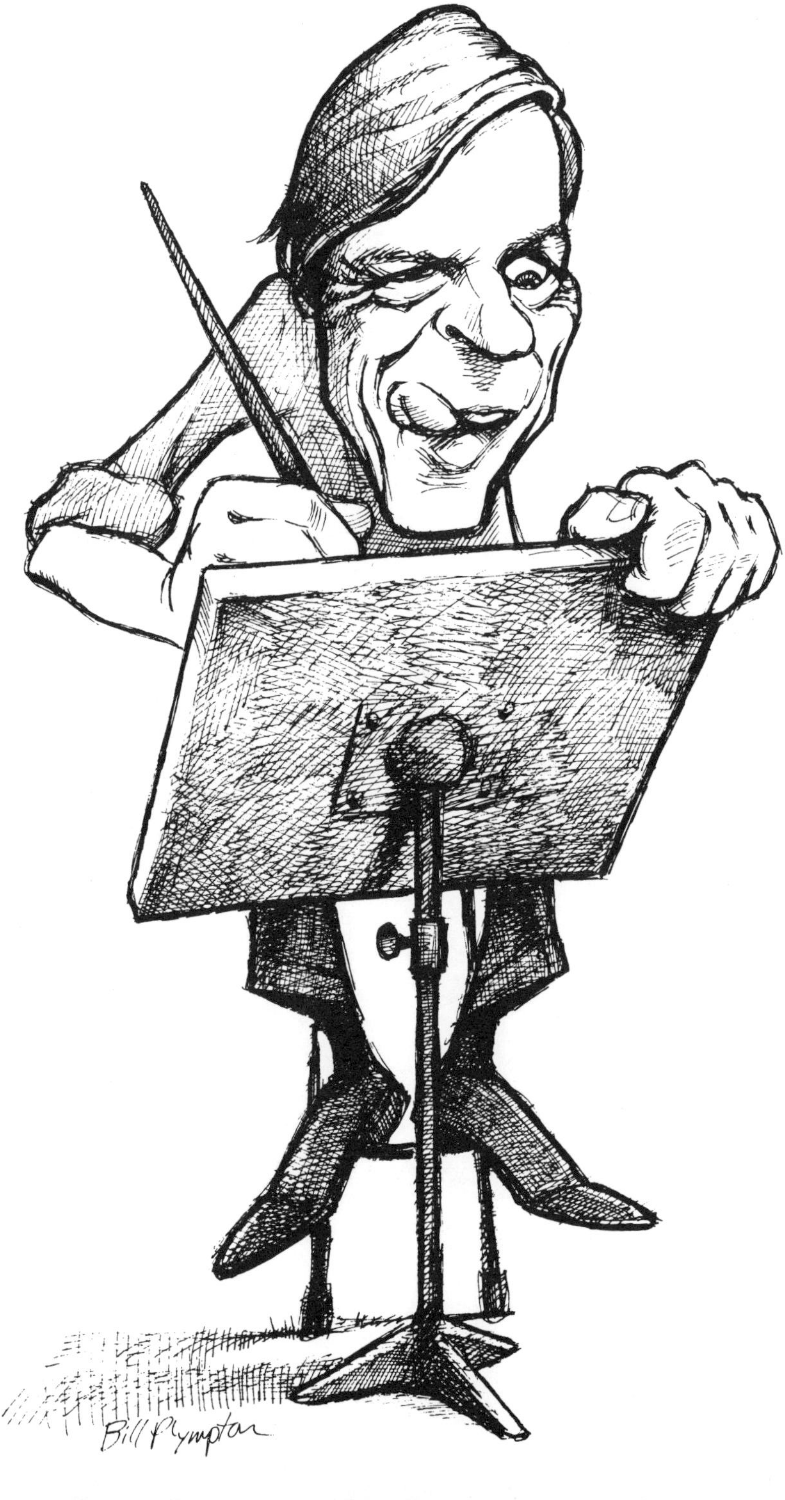
Bill Plympton

Introduction
by
George Plimpton

I have always envied those who practice the art of cartooning, and are good at it. The one drawing I ever had published—when I was the editor of the *Harvard Lampoon* and had the power to put in my own material—was printed upside down, a state which my staffers, who were probably responsible, assured me was an improvement on the original concept. Indeed, as I turned the magazine around a few times I was inclined to agree with them— though I did take exception to one of the *Lampoon* people who preferred the caricature lying on its side. Since that time I have become only slightly more proficient, as the drawings on the next page might indicate. In case the reader does not immediately recognize them as U.S. Presidents, I have identified which is which.

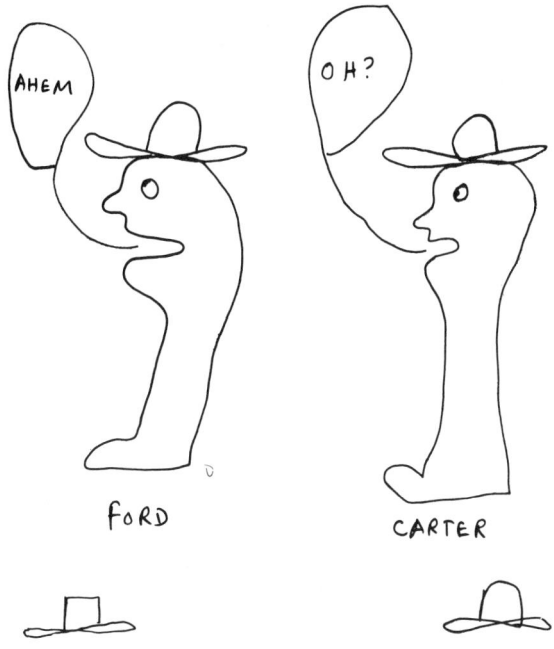

FORD

CARTER

The reader will notice my hats. I have trouble with the tops of my heads, so I invariably put hats on them. I am not bad at hats, and sometimes I draw them lying around at the feet of my caricatures (or rather the foot, since I am incapable of drawing a pair of legs on anyone *en profile*). It will be noticed that I am not all that bad at drawing the balloons to contain the words the cartoonist's characters have in mind to say. My trouble is with the words to put in the balloons—as is demonstrated by what I have my two Presidents saying . . . their comments lacking a certain *je ne sais quoi*.

All of this is preamble to an expression of my admiration for the craftsmanship and the wit of Bill Plympton. He is not only an admirable artist (he has no trouble with his legs at all) but he finds very funny and perceptive things for his people to say. How rare it is to find an artist adept at both these requirements of the great caricaturist-cartoonist. Some are good at finding things for their characters to say, but deliver them through uninspired child-like stick people; others are draughtsmen with skill but little wit. Plympton, on the other hand, combines artistic skills (some of his caricatures reflect a close study of Honoré Daumier) with a lively sense of his function as an artist-commentator in these parlous times—namely to present his work as a corrective to social inertia.

What follows is a selection of Bill's best strips and caricatures since 1975. Some of them ran originally in *The Soho Weekly News*, others in a small-press paperback titled *Tube Strips*. Many published here are new—an added fillip for those familiar with Bill's work as they commemorate the pleasure they first had at discovering it.

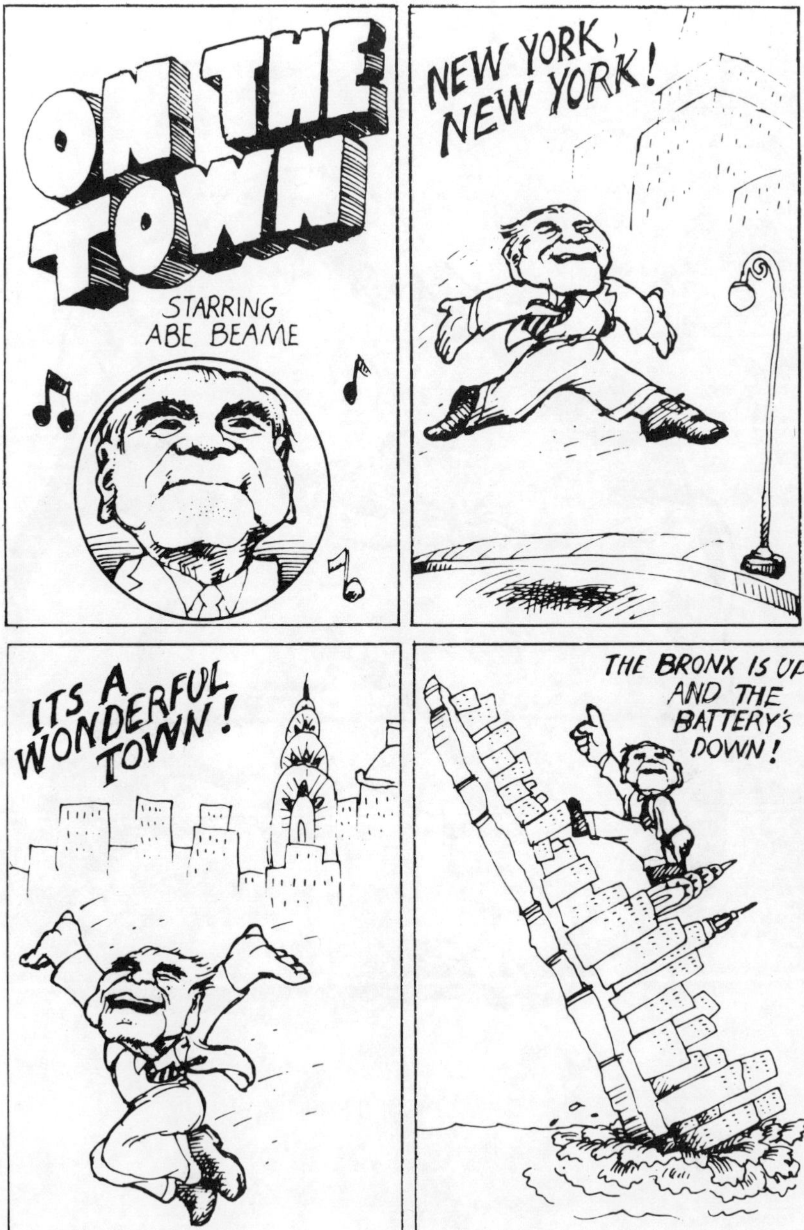
ON THE TOWN
STARRING ABE BEAME
NEW YORK, NEW YORK!
ITS A WONDERFUL TOWN!
THE BRONX IS UP AND THE BATTERY'S DOWN!
Bill Plympton © 75

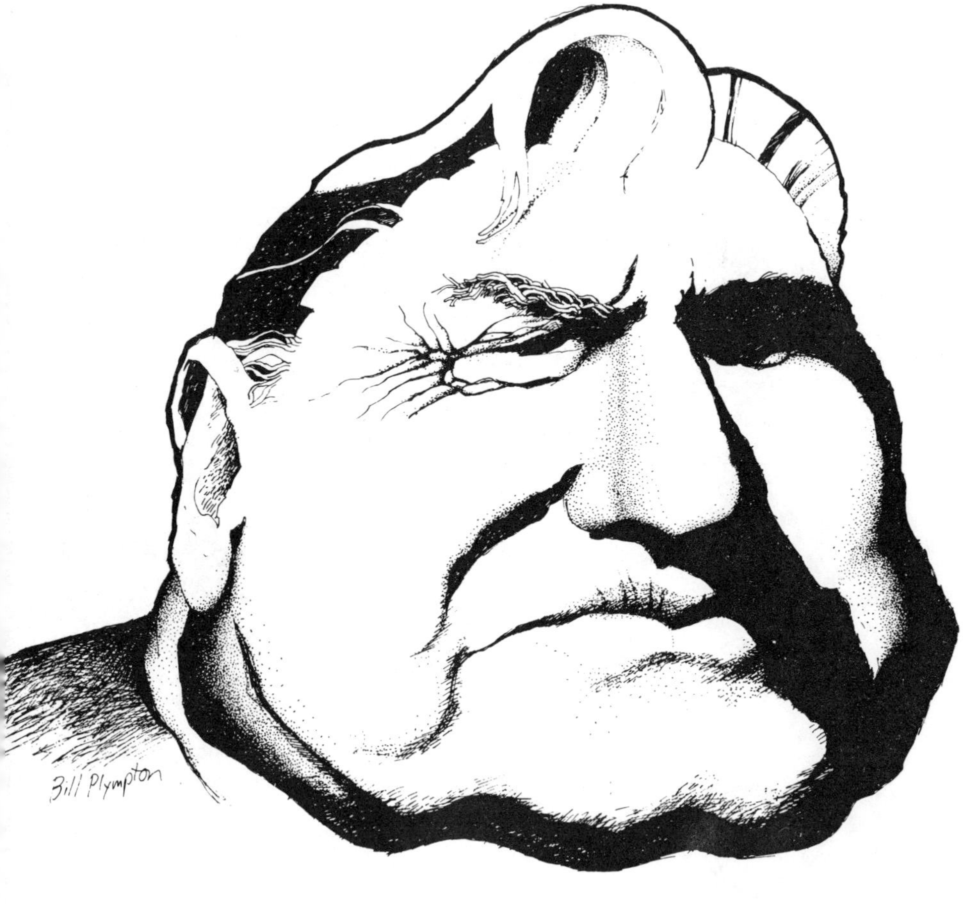
Bill Plympton

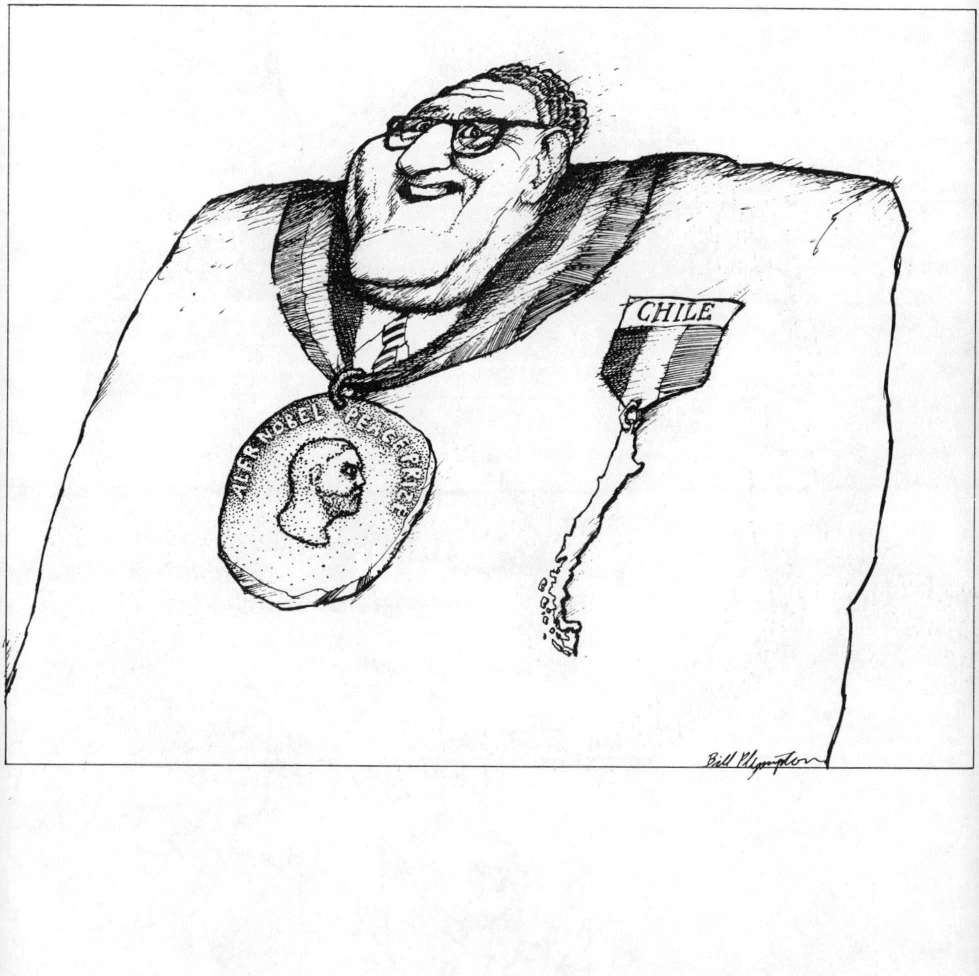
NOBEL
CHILE
Bill Plympton

HI YA! THIS IS NELSON ROCKEFELLER WITH SOME ENERGY TIPS.
DID YOU KNOW THAT IF EVERY AMERICAN LOWERED THEIR THERMOSTAT 5°...

COOKING WITH KISSINGER
TODAY VE LEARN HOW TO MAKE CHILI HOT!
FIRST VE ADD SOME UNION STRIKES AND SOME PAID OFF SENATORS

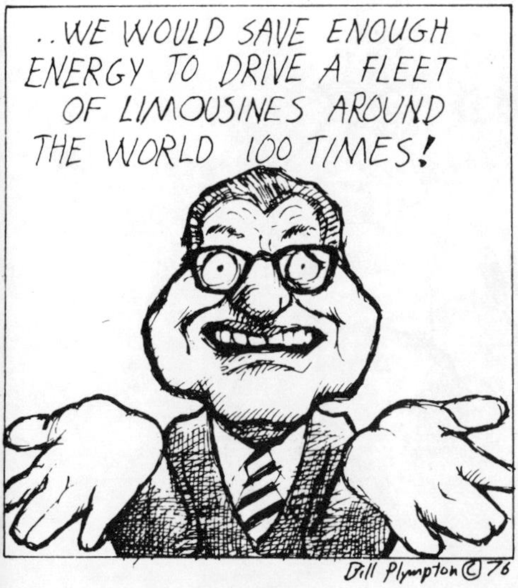
..WE WOULD SAVE ENOUGH ENERGY TO DRIVE A FLEET OF LIMOUSINES AROUND THE WORLD 100 TIMES!
Bill Plympton © 76

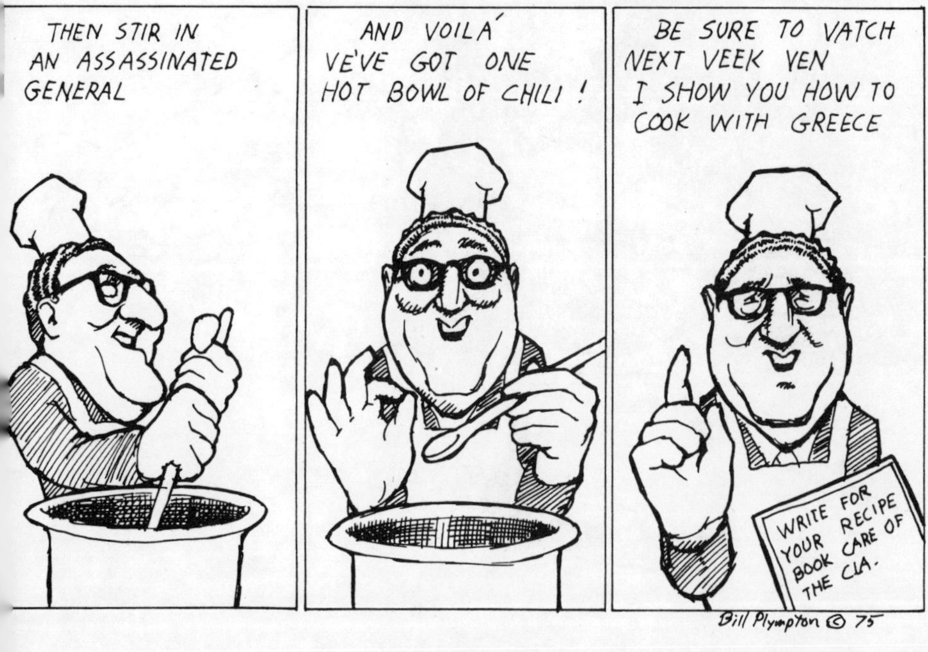
THEN STIR IN AN ASSASSINATED GENERAL
AND VOILÁ VE'VE GOT ONE HOT BOWL OF CHILI!
BE SURE TO VATCH NEXT VEEK VEN I SHOW YOU HOW TO COOK WITH GREECE
WRITE FOR YOUR RECIPE BOOK CARE OF THE CIA.
Bill Plympton © 75

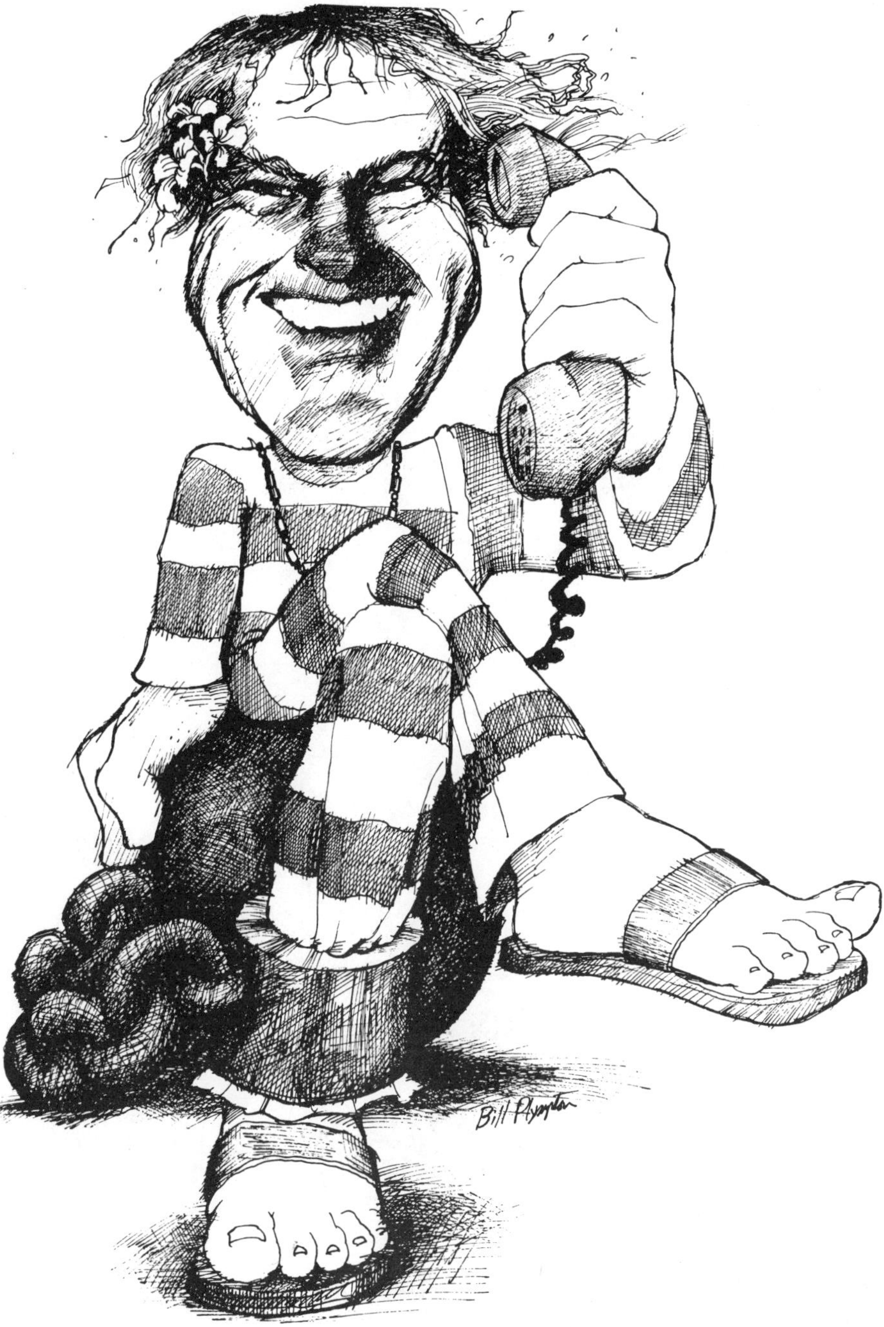
Bill Plympton

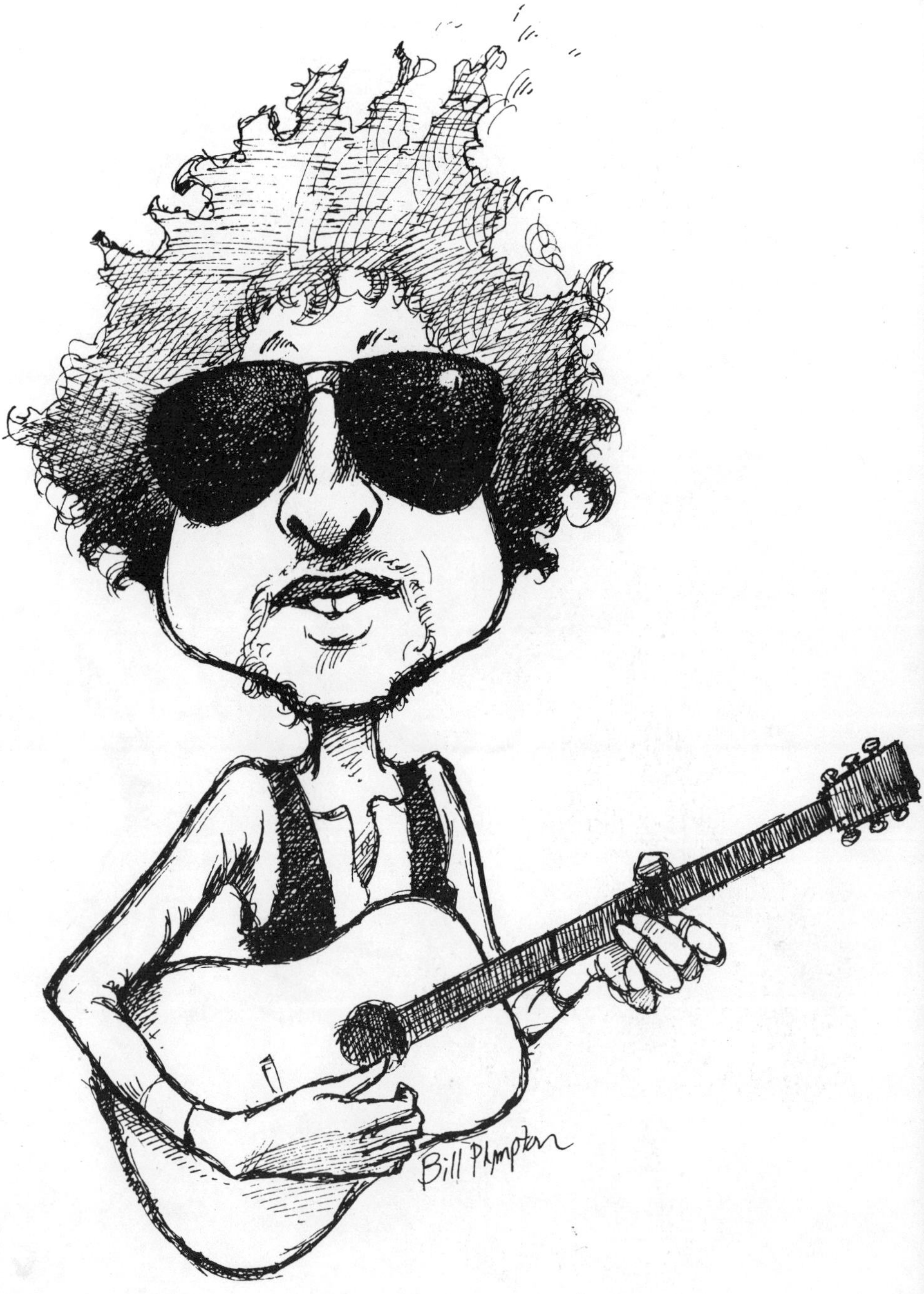
Bill Plympton

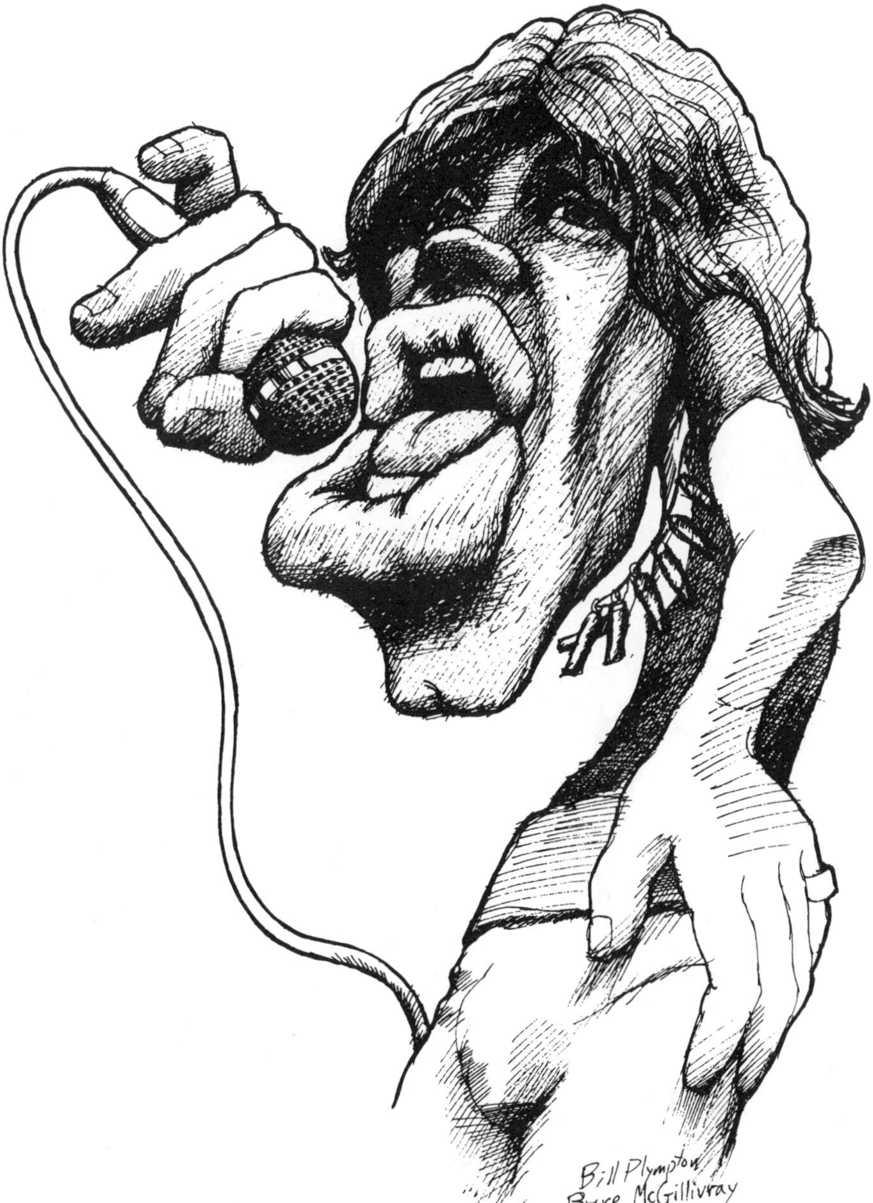
Bill Plympton
Bruce McGillivray

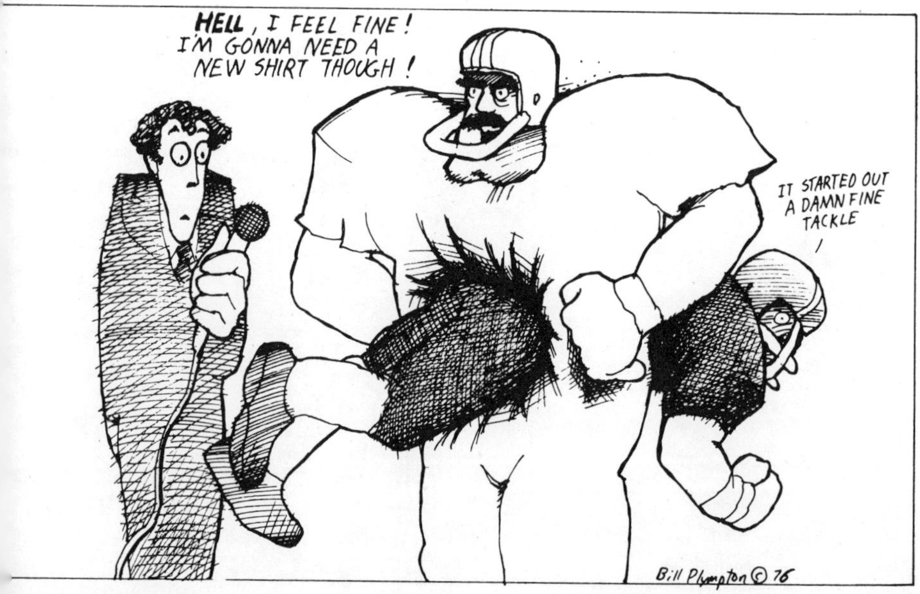
HELL, I FEEL FINE! I'M GONNA NEED A NEW SHIRT THOUGH!
IT STARTED OUT A DAMN FINE TACKLE
Bill Plympton © 76

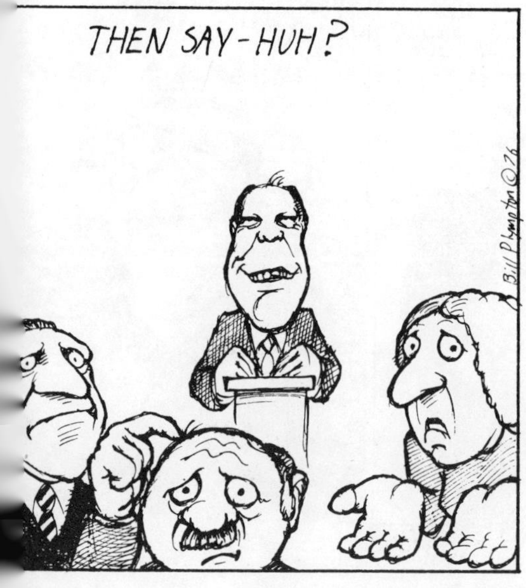
THEN SAY-HUH?
Bill Plympton © 76

HELLO - I'M EDWIN NEWMAN - AND TODAY WITH ME SPEAKING FREELY IS THE LIGHT AT THE END OF THE TUNNEL ....

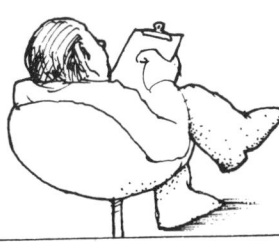

GOOD AFTERNOON! - IS IT TRUE THAT IN VIETNAM THERE IN FACT, WAS NO END OF THE TUNNEL - AND THAT YOU WERE USED TO PROLONG THE WAR?

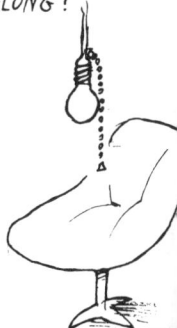

LIES! LIES! I WAS JUST STANDING IN TILL THE REAL END OF THE TUNNEL CAME ALONG!

HI, THIS IS "DUKE" WAYNE IF YOU'RE UNEMPLOYED AND LOOKING FOR A JOB WITH BALLS - I'VE GOT THE ANSWER - M.T.I.

MERCENARY TRAINING INSTITUTE

TELL ME - NOW THAT THE WAR IS OVER WHAT ARE YOUR FUTURE PLANS?
WELL ED - THERE'S ALWAYS WORK FOR GOOD LIGHTS AT THE END OF TUNNELS - IN FACT PRESIDENT FORD WANTS ME TO HELP HIM OUT WITH THIS RECESSION THING.
Bill Plympton

THATS RIGHT, YOU CAN LEARN MILITARY TECHNIQUES RIGHT IN THE PRIVACY OF YOUR OWN HOME.
AND WE CAN GUARANTEE IMMEDIATE JOBS. JUST CONTACT OUR PLACEMENT OFFICE - IN ANGOLA.
Bill Plympton © '75

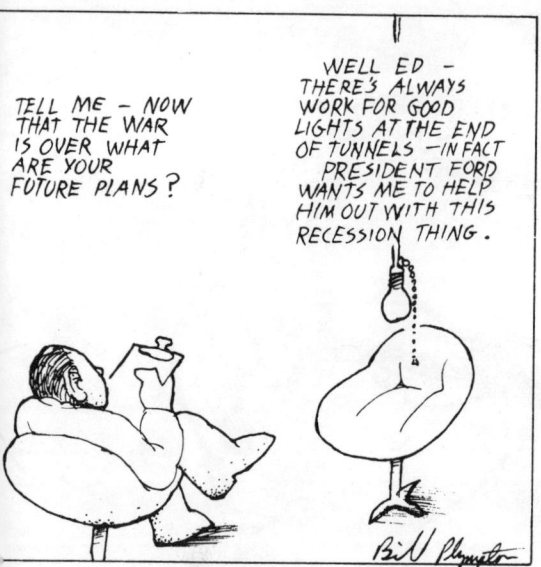

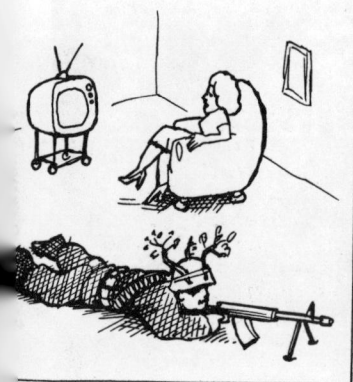

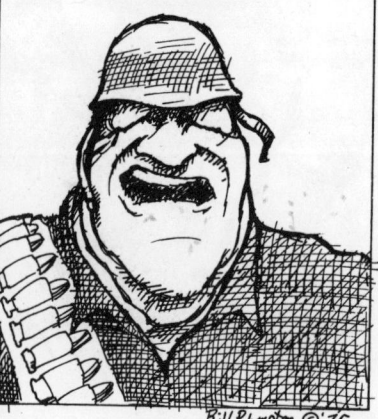

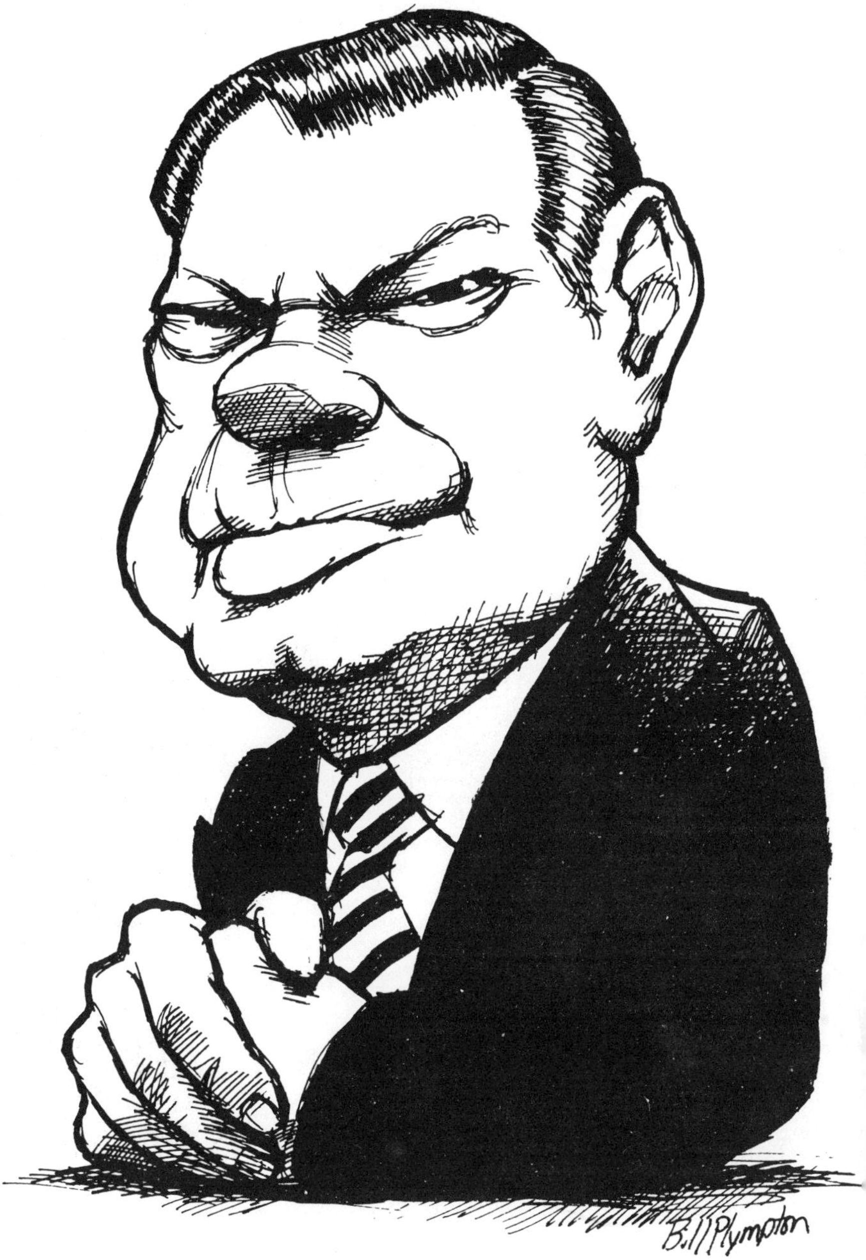

Bill Plympton

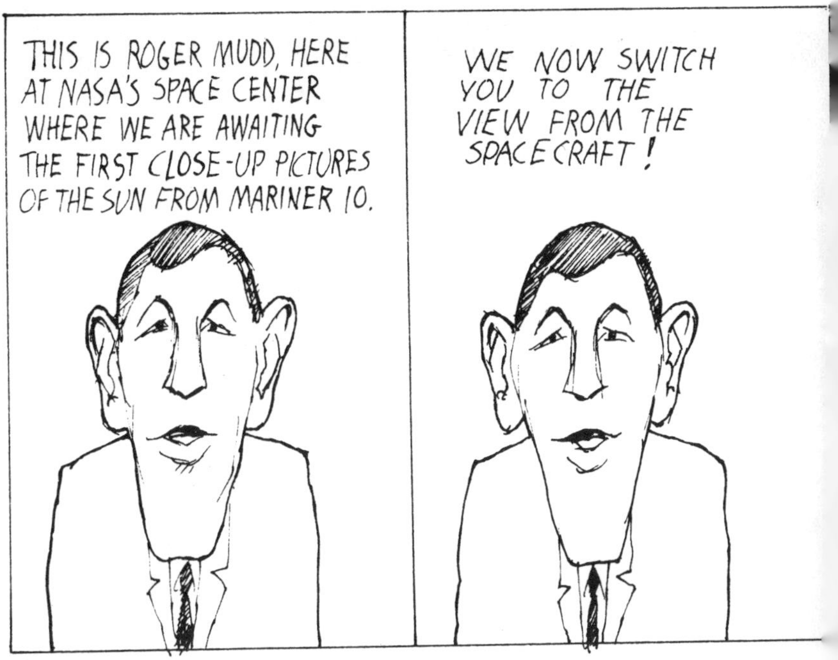
THIS IS ROGER MUDD, HERE AT NASA'S SPACE CENTER WHERE WE ARE AWAITING THE FIRST CLOSE-UP PICTURES OF THE SUN FROM MARINER 10.
WE NOW SWITCH YOU TO THE VIEW FROM THE SPACECRAFT!

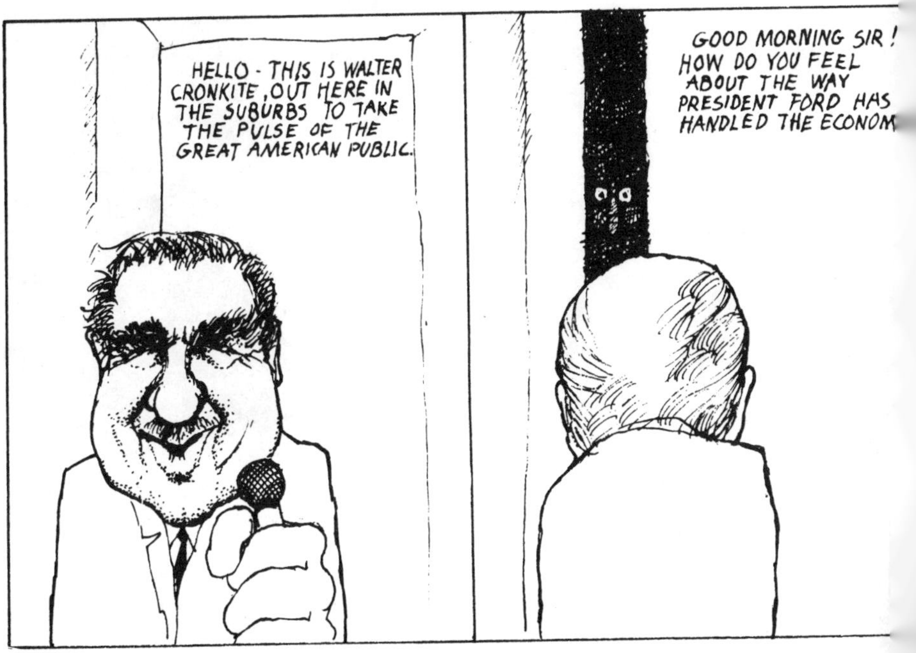
HELLO - THIS IS WALTER CRONKITE, OUT HERE IN THE SUBURBS TO TAKE THE PULSE OF THE GREAT AMERICAN PUBLIC.
GOOD MORNING SIR! HOW DO YOU FEEL ABOUT THE WAY PRESIDENT FORD HAS HANDLED THE ECONOM

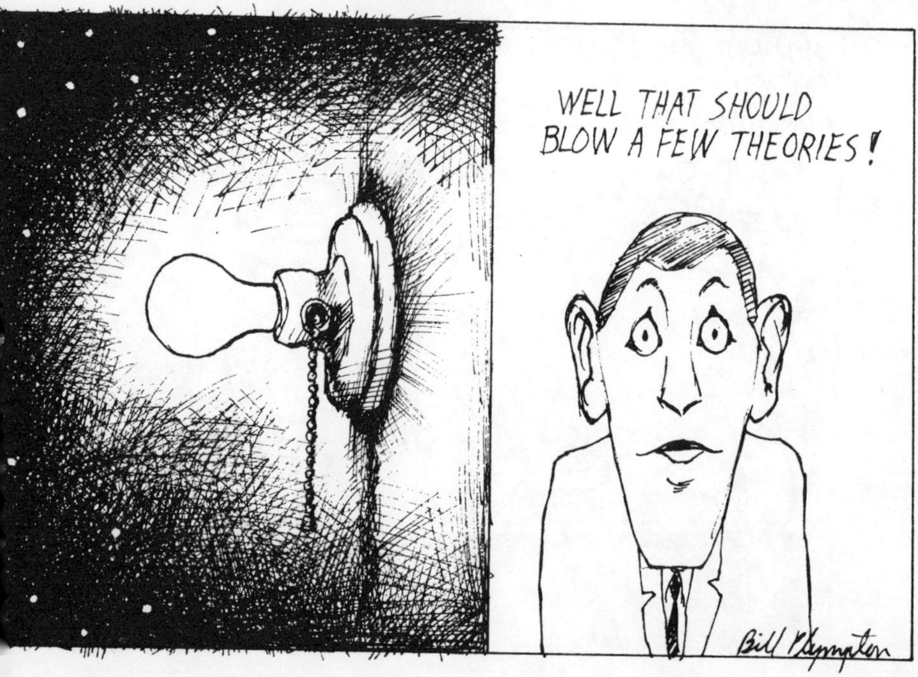
WELL THAT SHOULD
BLOW A FEW THEORIES!
Bill Plympton

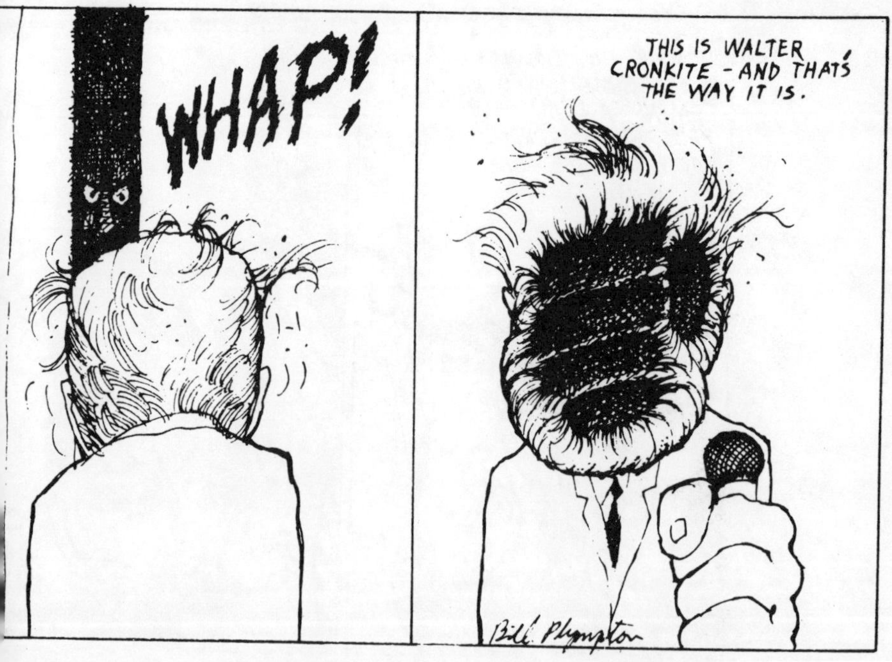
WHAP!
THIS IS WALTER CRONKITE - AND THAT'S THE WAY IT IS.
Bill Plympton

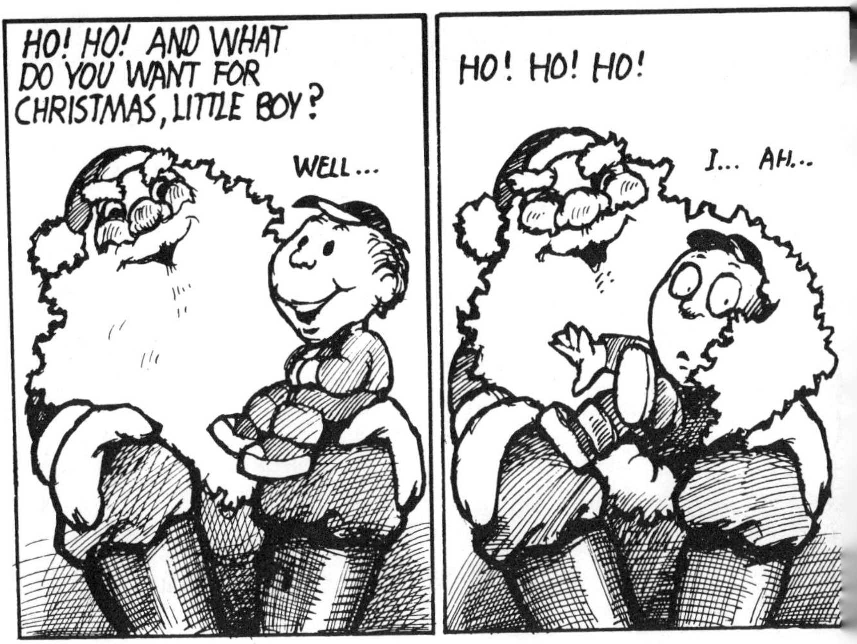
HO! HO! AND WHAT DO YOU WANT FOR CHRISTMAS, LITTLE BOY?
WELL...
HO! HO! HO!
I... AH...

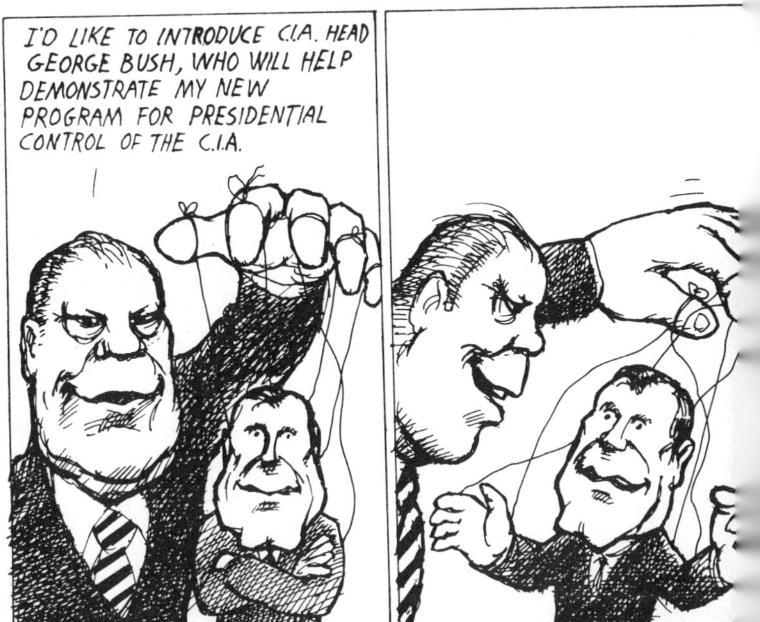
I'D LIKE TO INTRODUCE C.I.A. HEAD GEORGE BUSH, WHO WILL HELP DEMONSTRATE MY NEW PROGRAM FOR PRESIDENTIAL CONTROL OF THE C.I.A.

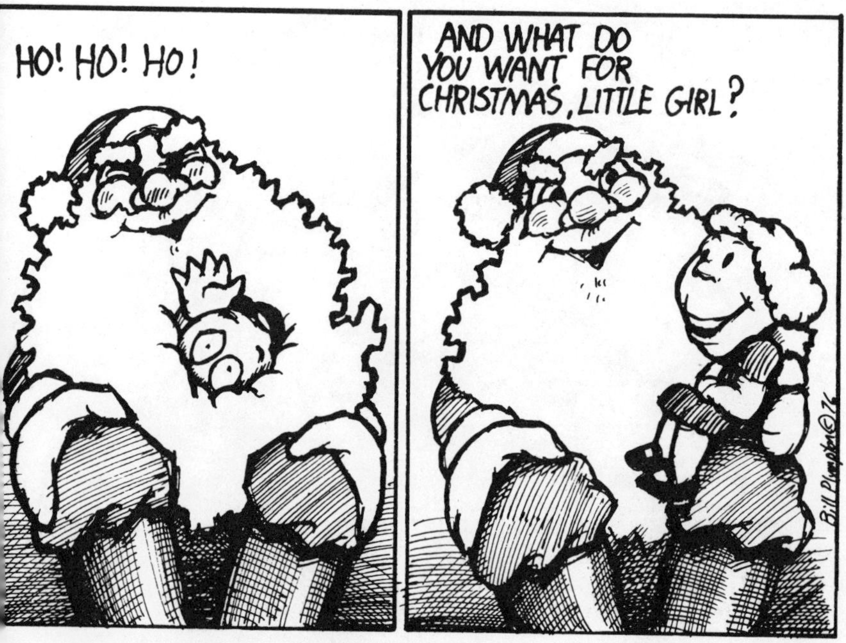
HO! HO! HO!
AND WHAT DO YOU WANT FOR CHRISTMAS, LITTLE GIRL?
Bill Plympton © 76

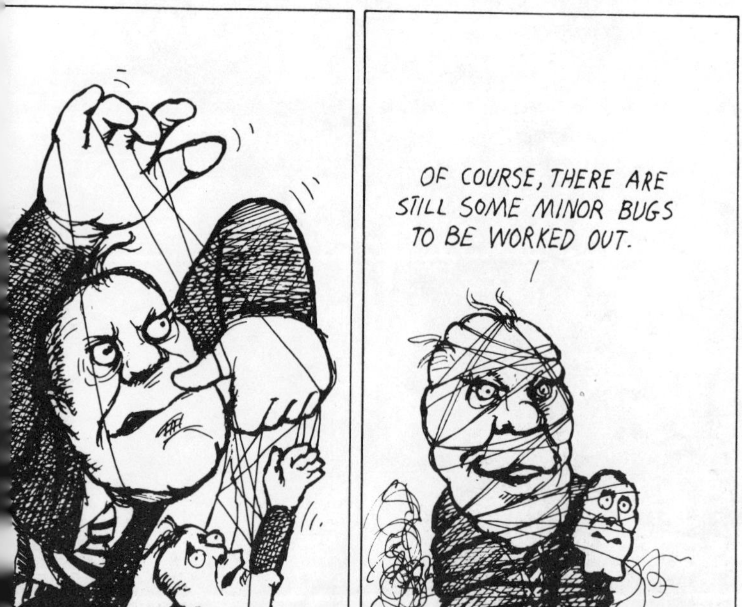
OF COURSE, THERE ARE STILL SOME MINOR BUGS TO BE WORKED OUT.
Bill Plympton © 76

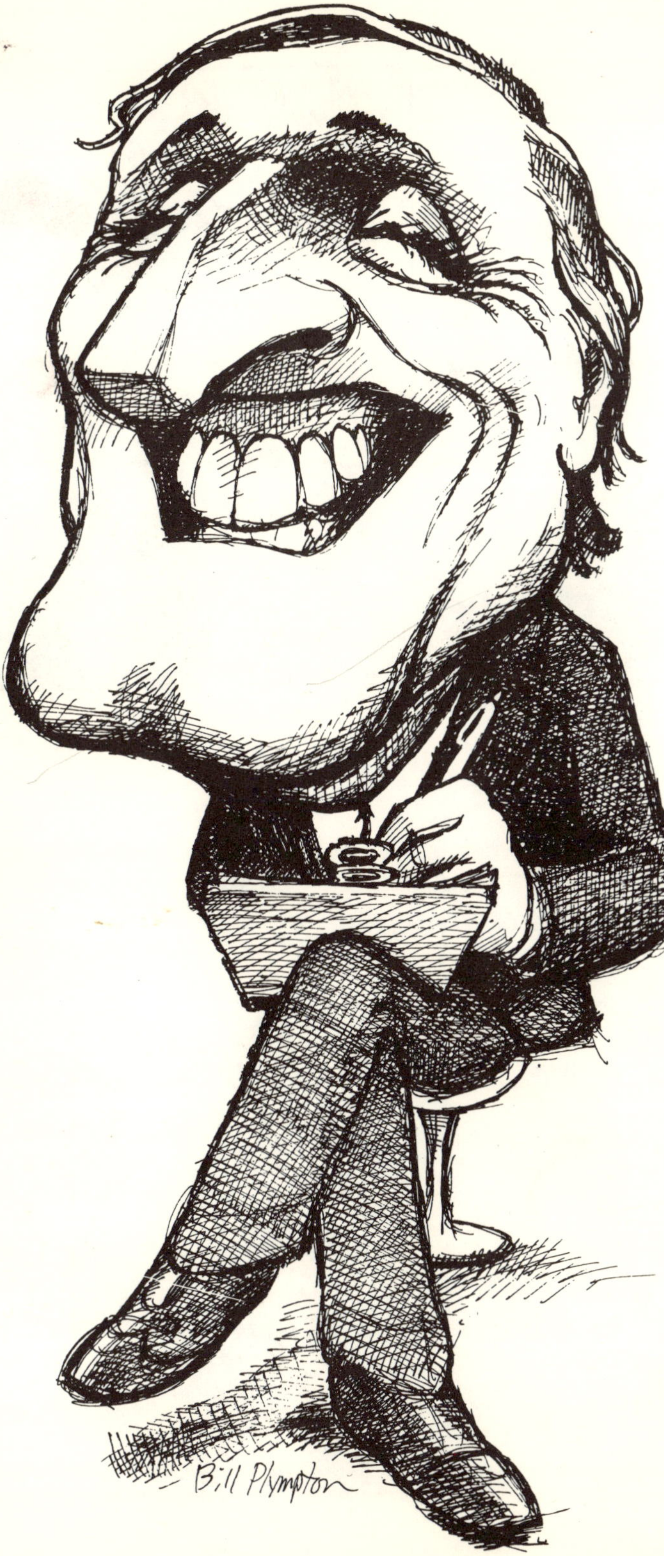
Bill Plympton

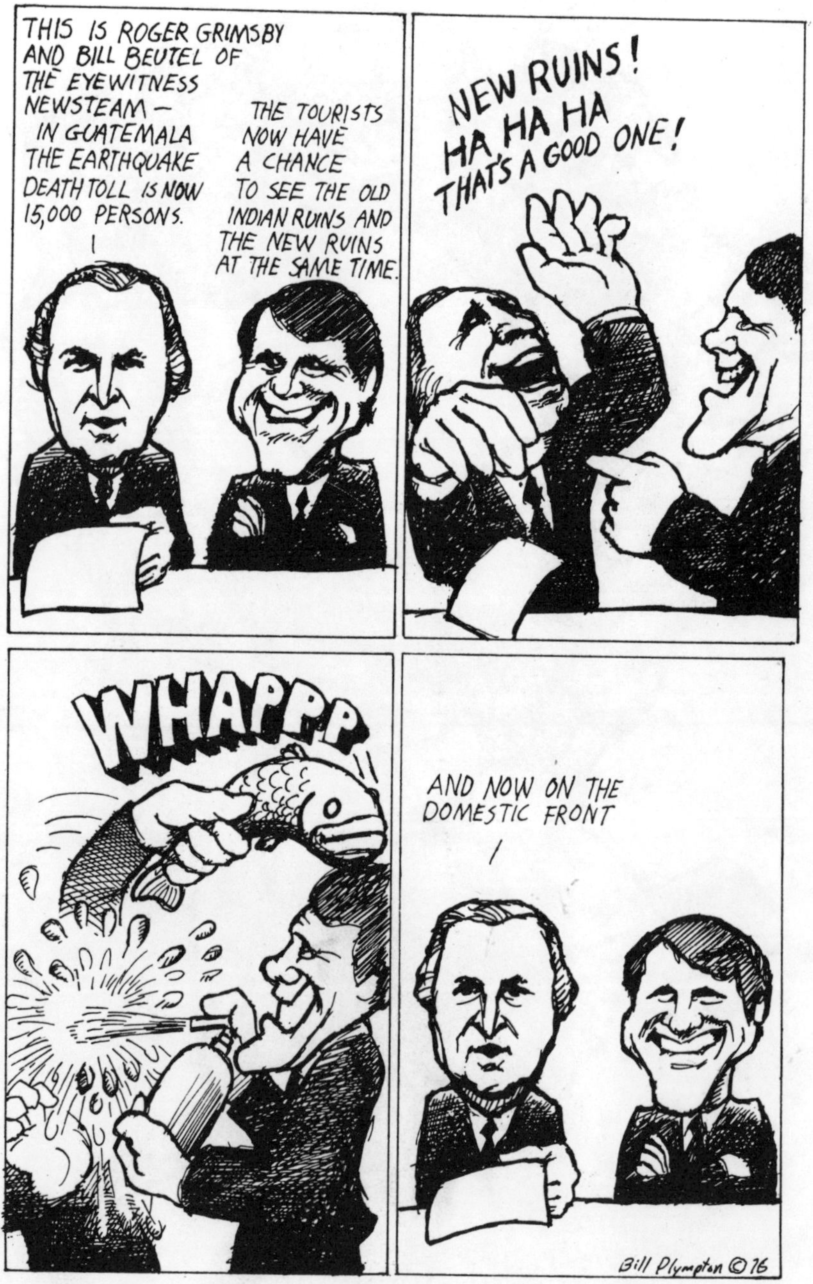

THIS IS ROGER GRIMSBY AND BILL BEUTEL OF THE EYEWITNESS NEWSTEAM — IN GUATEMALA THE EARTHQUAKE DEATH TOLL IS NOW 15,000 PERSONS.
THE TOURISTS NOW HAVE A CHANCE TO SEE THE OLD INDIAN RUINS AND THE NEW RUINS AT THE SAME TIME.
NEW RUINS! HA HA HA THAT'S A GOOD ONE!
WHAPPP
AND NOW ON THE DOMESTIC FRONT
Bill Plympton ©76

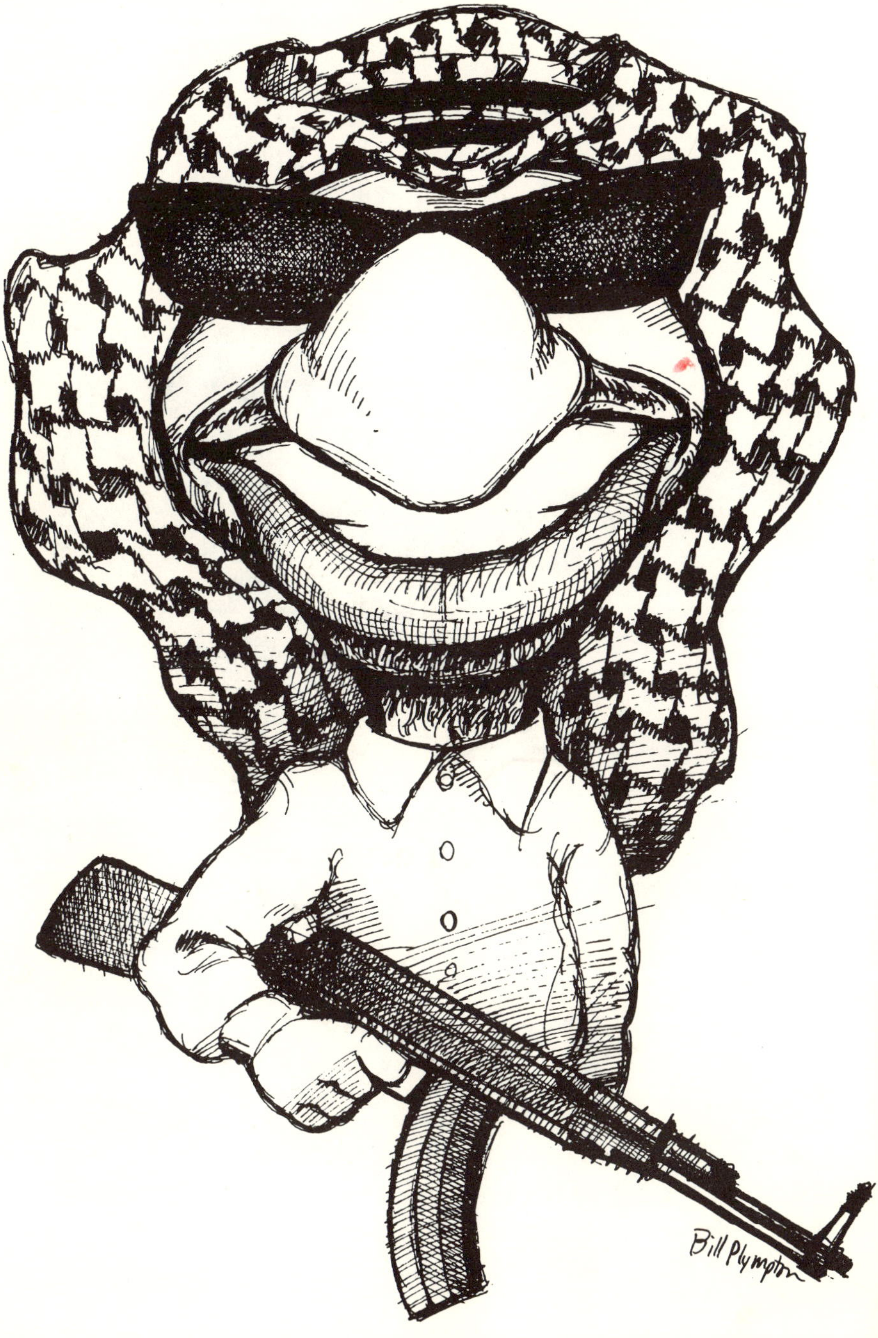
Bill Plympton

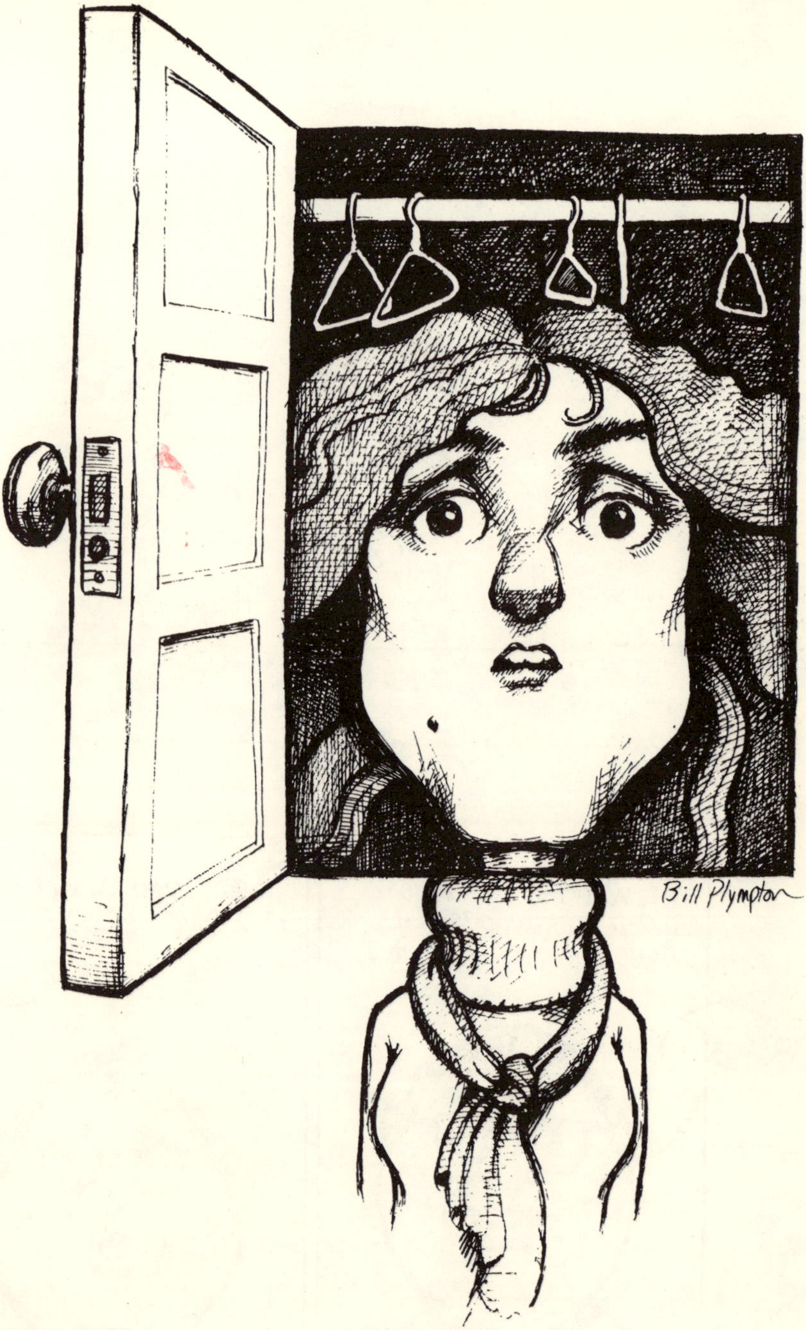

Bill Plympton

MR. PRESIDENT DO YOU BLAME CONGRESS FOR THE LOSS OF SOUTH VIETNAM?
I AM NOT ASSESSING BLAME ON ANYONE.
I THINK HISTORIANS IN THE FUTURE WILL WRITE WHO IS TO BLAME.

HELLO, I'M CHUCK COLSON. I WAS THE ONE WHO VOWED TO RUN OVER HIS GRANDMOTHER FOR NIXON.
WELL THAT WAS THE OLD CHUCK COLSON.

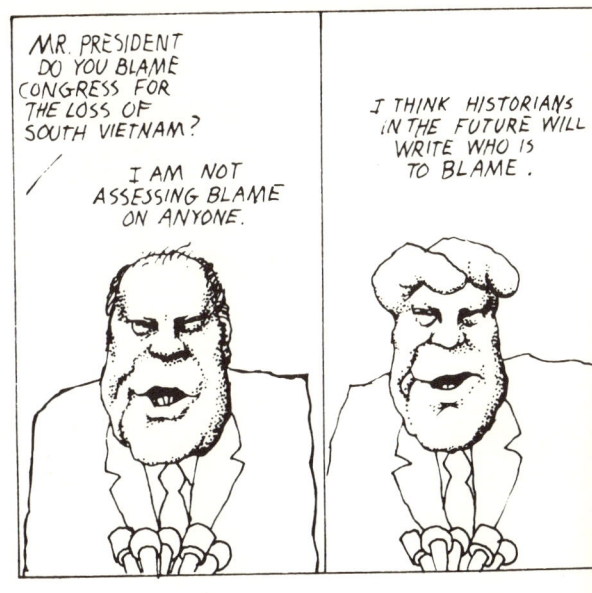

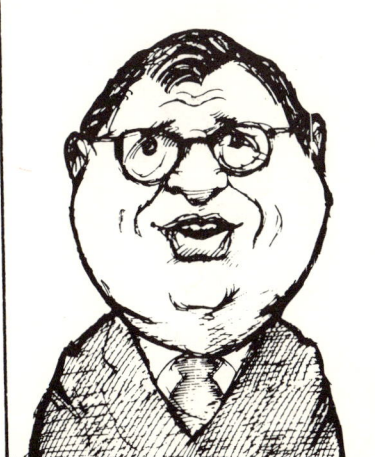

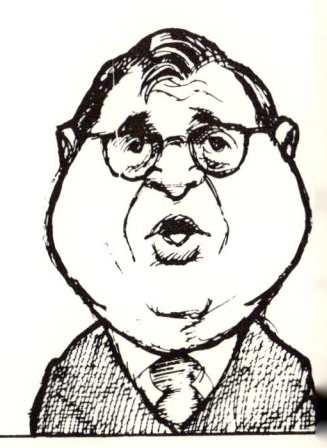

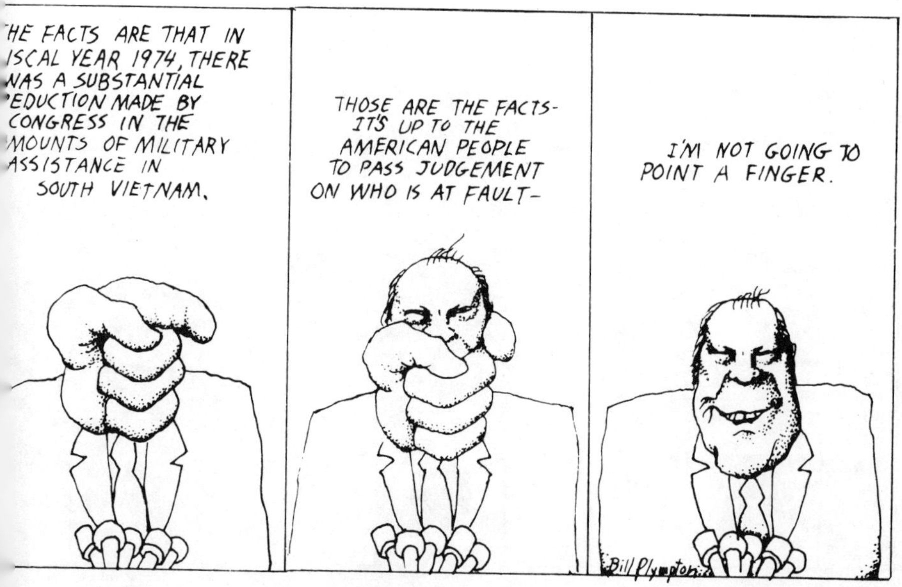
HE FACTS ARE THAT IN
ISCAL YEAR 1974, THERE
NAS A SUBSTANTIAL
EDUCTION MADE BY
CONGRESS IN THE
MOUNTS OF MILITARY
ASSISTANCE IN
SOUTH VIETNAM.
THOSE ARE THE FACTS-
IT'S UP TO THE
AMERICAN PEOPLE
TO PASS JUDGEMENT
ON WHO IS AT FAULT-
I'M NOT GOING TO
POINT A FINGER.
Bill Plympton

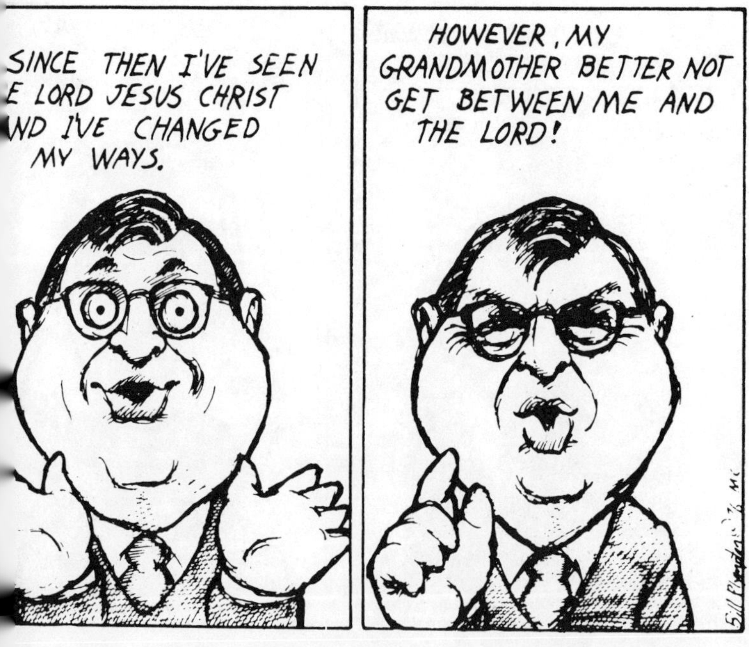
SINCE THEN I'VE SEEN
E LORD JESUS CHRIST
ND I'VE CHANGED
MY WAYS.
HOWEVER, MY
GRANDMOTHER BETTER NOT
GET BETWEEN ME AND
THE LORD!

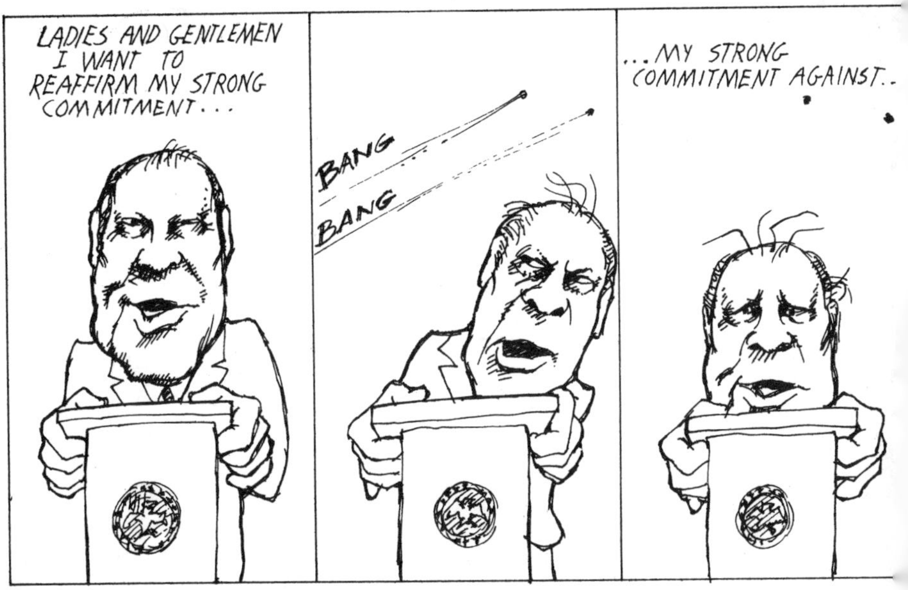
LADIES AND GENTLEMEN I WANT TO REAFFIRM MY STRONG COMMITMENT . . .
BANG
BANG
. . . MY STRONG COMMITMENT AGAINST . .

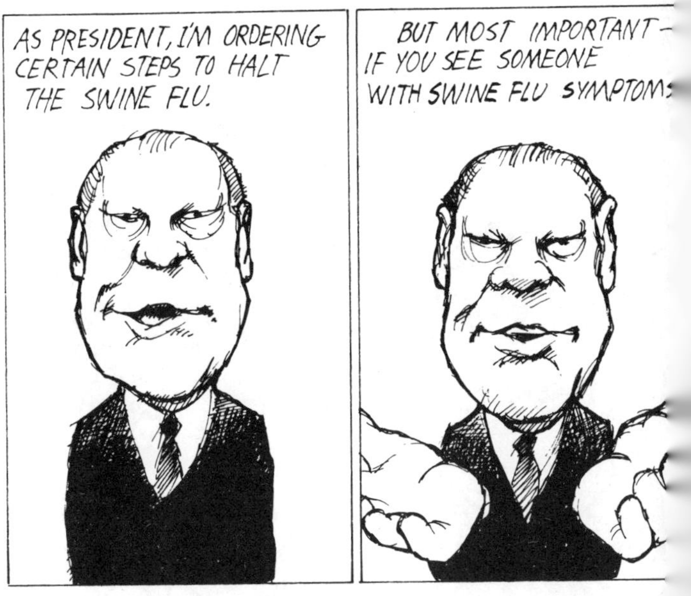
AS PRESIDENT, I'M ORDERING CERTAIN STEPS TO HALT THE SWINE FLU.
BUT MOST IMPORTANT — IF YOU SEE SOMEONE WITH SWINE FLU SYMPTOMS

BANG
BANG
BANG
...AGAINST GUN CONTROL — THANK YOU.
BANG
BANG
BANG
BANG
BANG
Bill Plympton © 1975

BE SURE TO REPORT
HEM TO HEALTH
OFFICIALS.
EYBDA ... EYBDA .. EYBDA
THAT'S ALL FOLKS !
Bill Plympton © 76

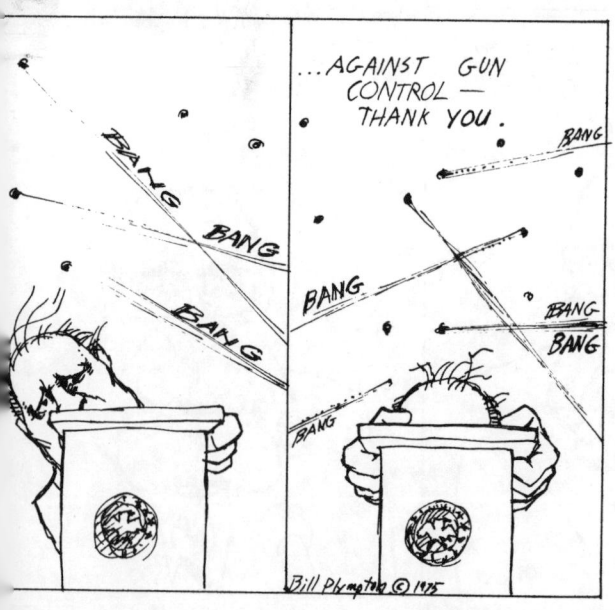

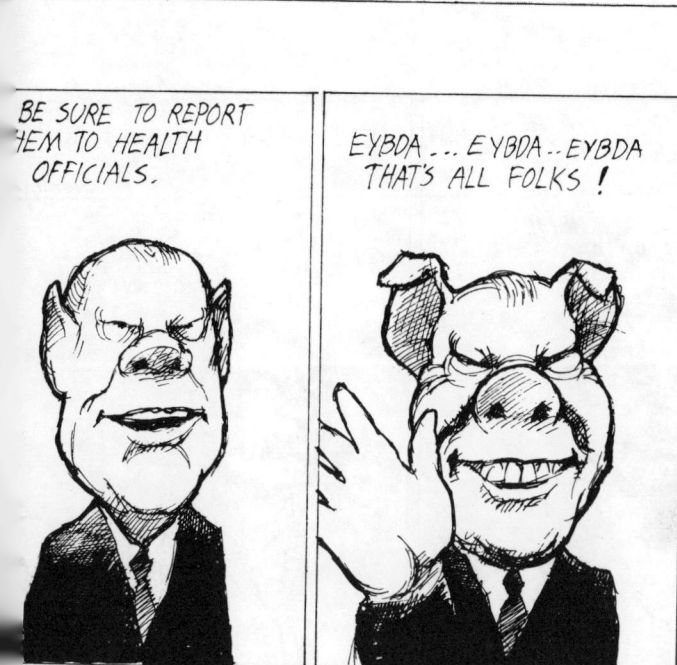

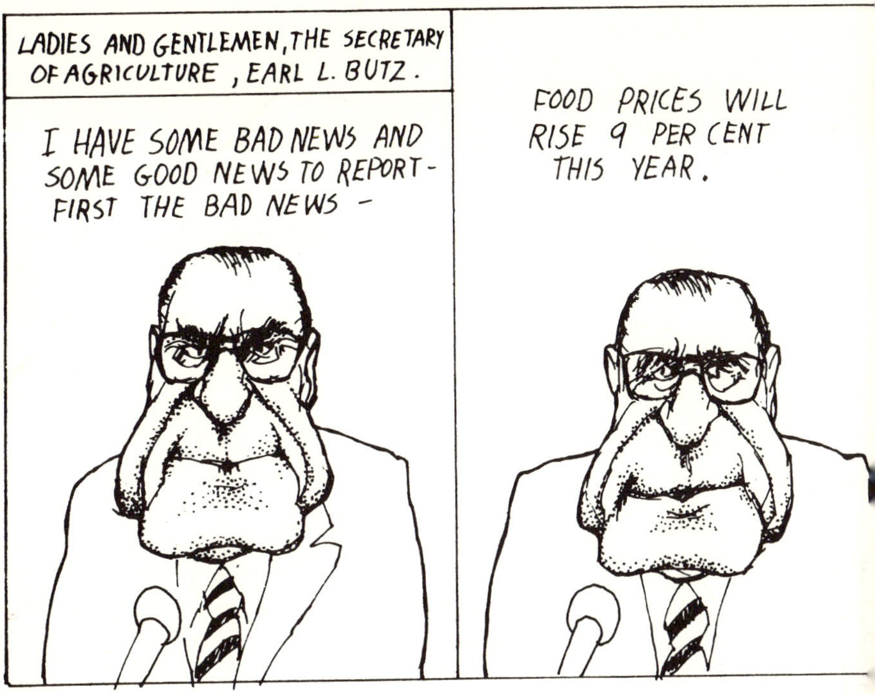
LADIES AND GENTLEMEN, THE SECRETARY OF AGRICULTURE, EARL L. BUTZ.
I HAVE SOME BAD NEWS AND SOME GOOD NEWS TO REPORT - FIRST THE BAD NEWS -
FOOD PRICES WILL RISE 9 PER CENT THIS YEAR.

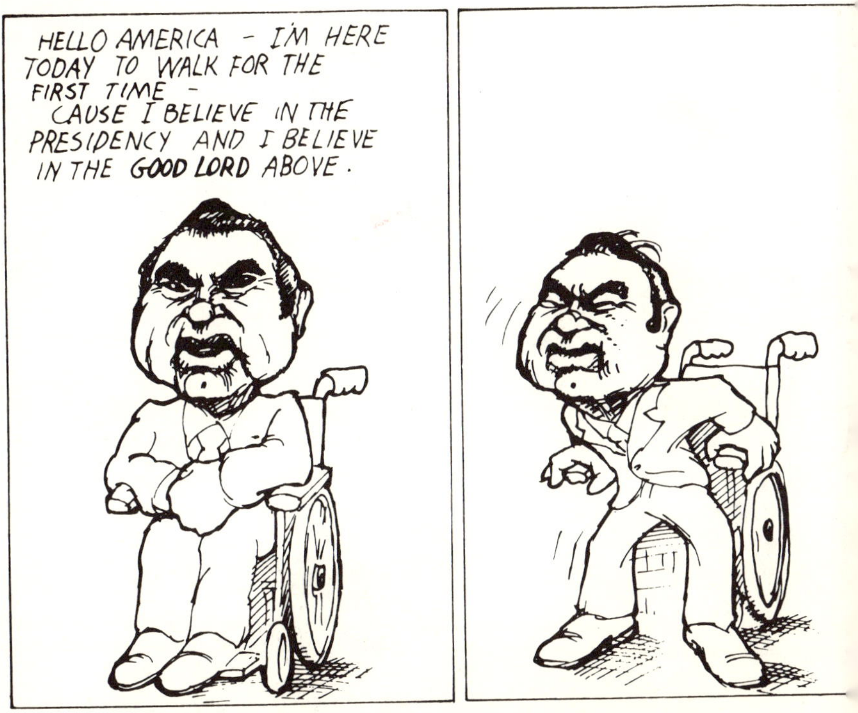
HELLO AMERICA - I'M HERE TODAY TO WALK FOR THE FIRST TIME - CAUSE I BELIEVE IN THE PRESIDENCY AND I BELIEVE IN THE GOOD LORD ABOVE.

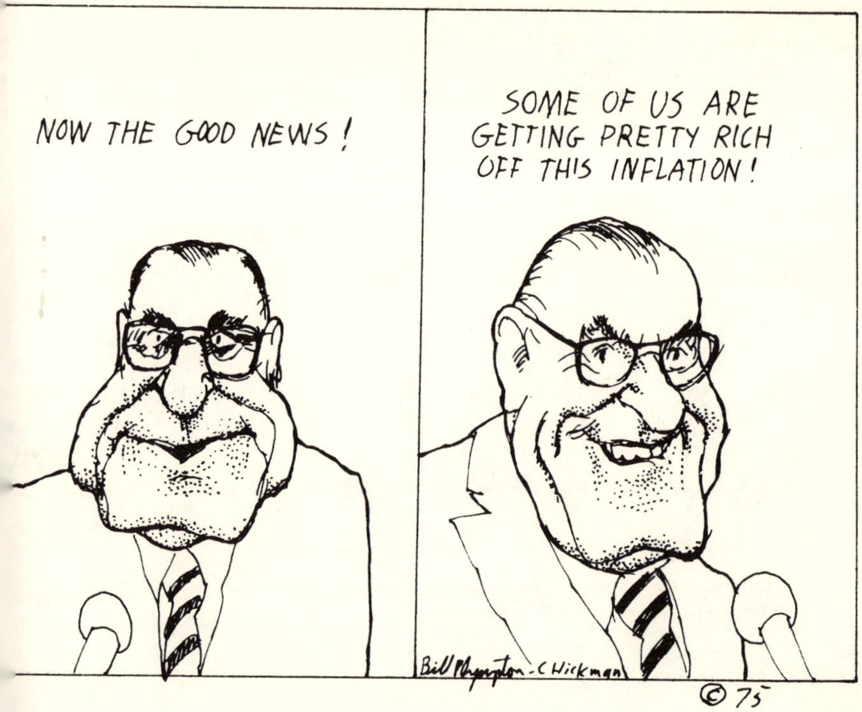
NOW THE GOOD NEWS!
SOME OF US ARE GETTING PRETTY RICH OFF THIS INFLATION!
Bill Plympton - C Hickman
© 75

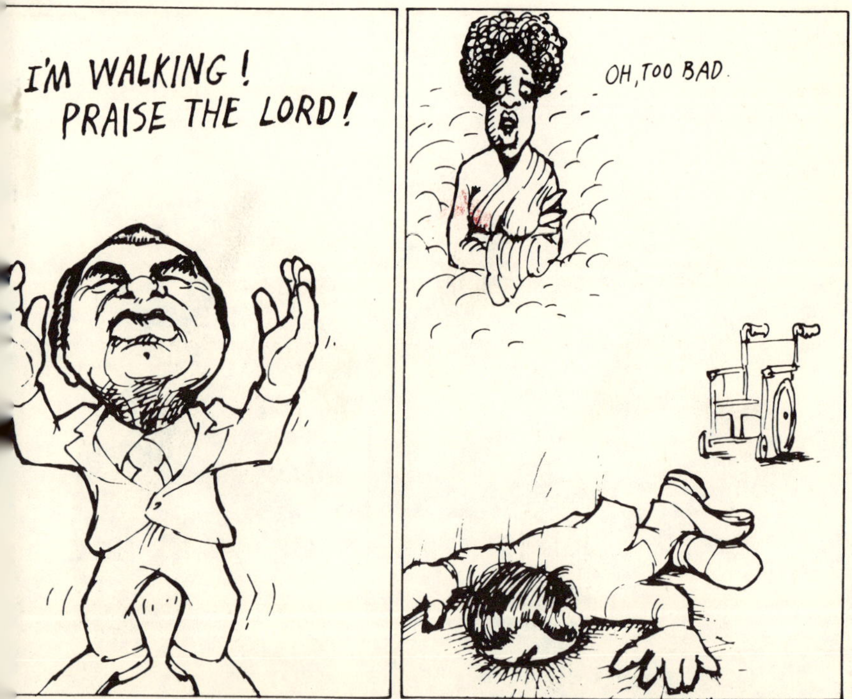
I'M WALKING! PRAISE THE LORD!
OH, TOO BAD.
© 75 Bill Plympton / B Cohen

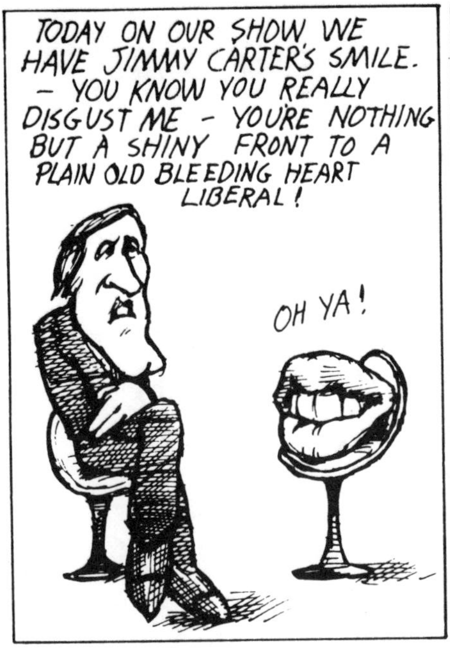
TODAY ON OUR SHOW WE HAVE JIMMY CARTER'S SMILE. – YOU KNOW YOU REALLY DISGUST ME – YOU'RE NOTHING BUT A SHINY FRONT TO A PLAIN OLD BLEEDING HEART LIBERAL!
OH YA!

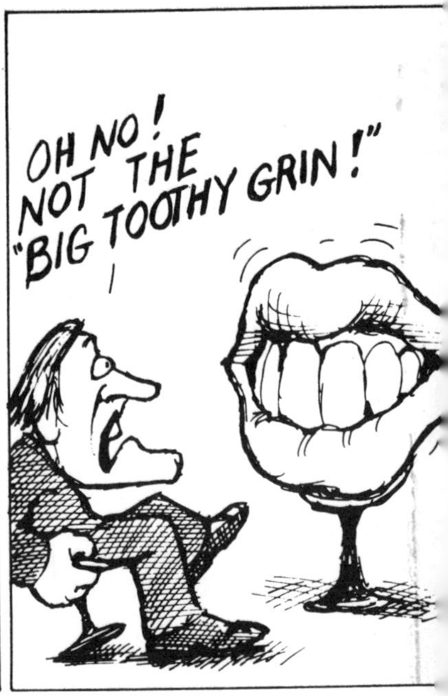
OH NO! NOT THE "BIG TOOTHY GRIN!"

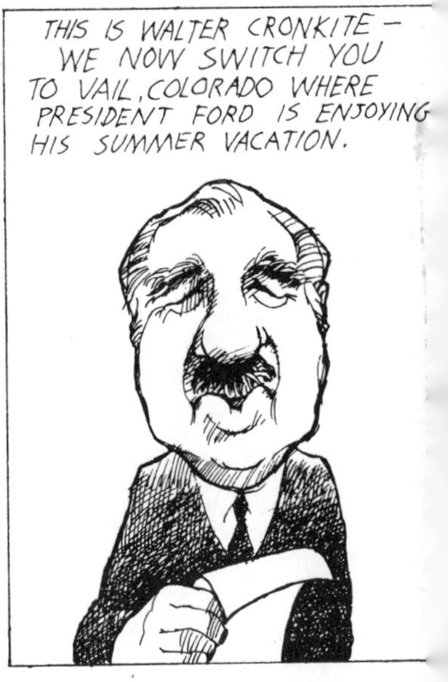
THIS IS WALTER CRONKITE – WE NOW SWITCH YOU TO VAIL, COLORADO WHERE PRESIDENT FORD IS ENJOYING HIS SUMMER VACATION.

ANYTHING-
STOP IT
STOP IT
STOP IT
THE "BIG TOOTHY GRIN" STRIKES AGAIN!
Bill Plympton © 76

Bill Plympton © 76

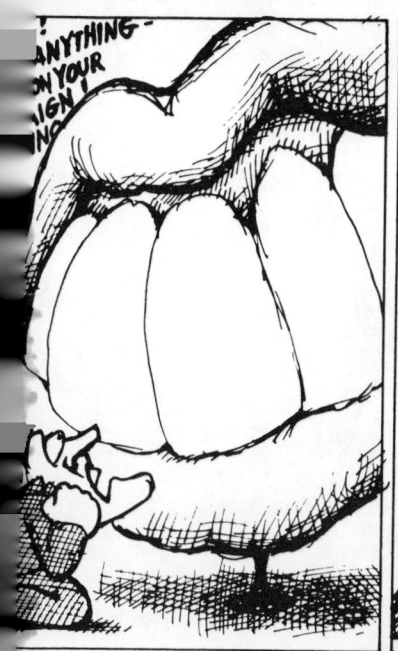

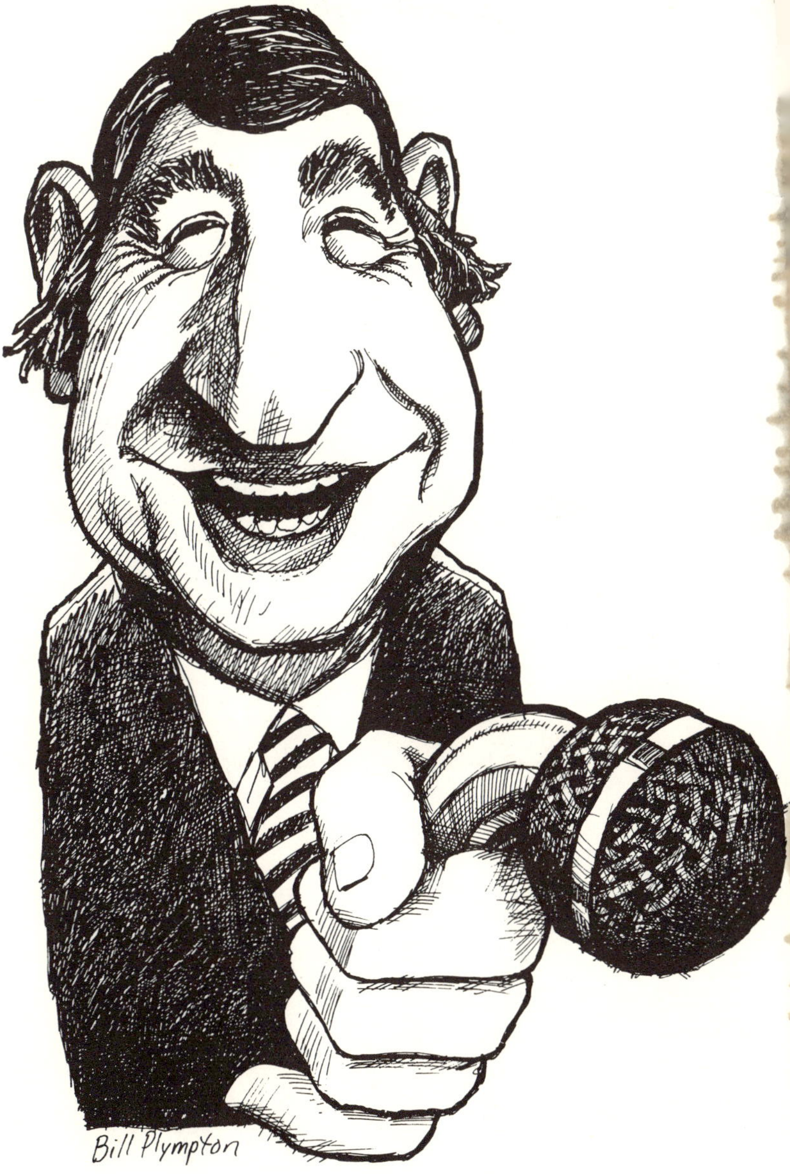
Bill Plympton

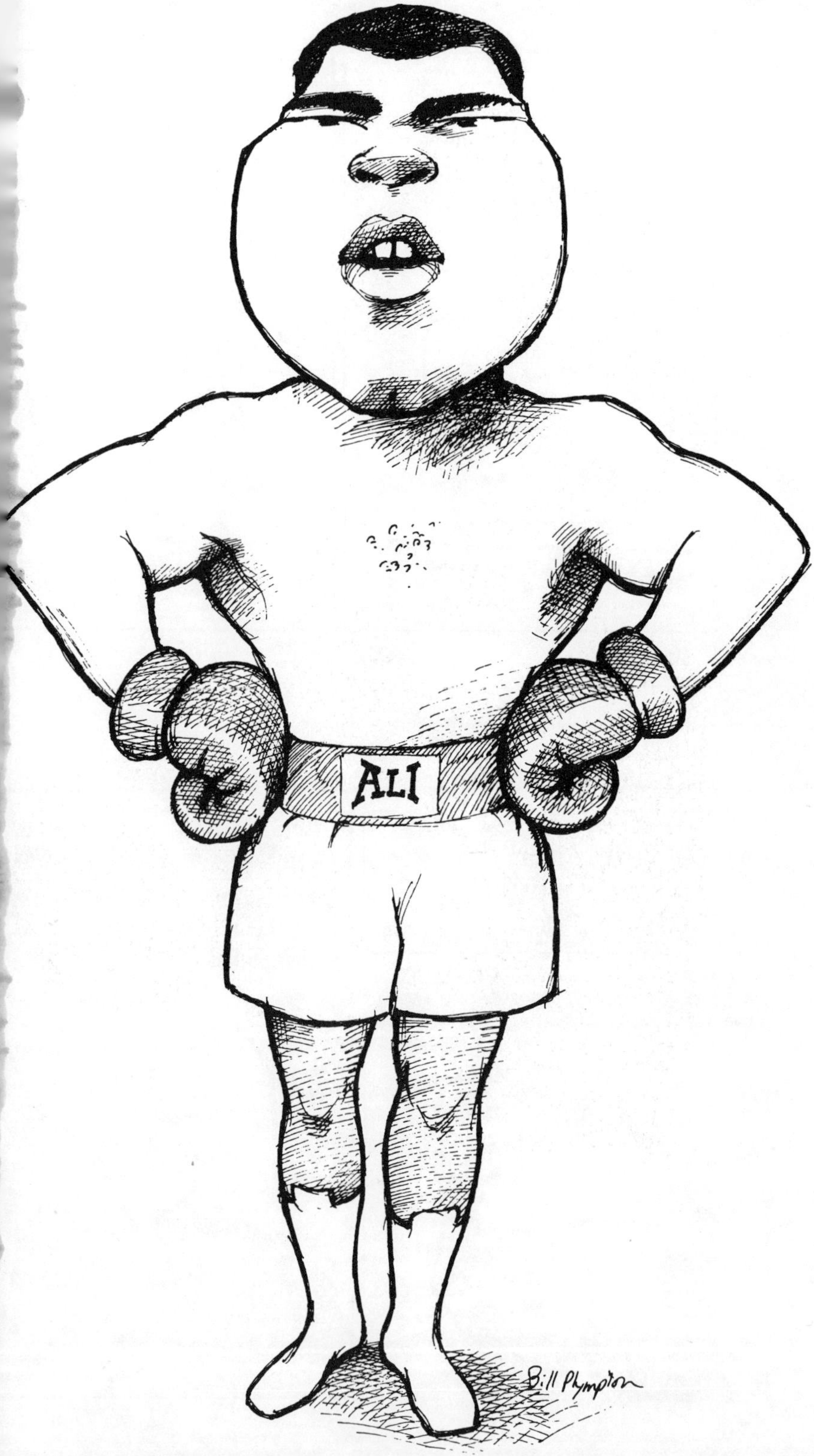
ALI
Bill Plympton

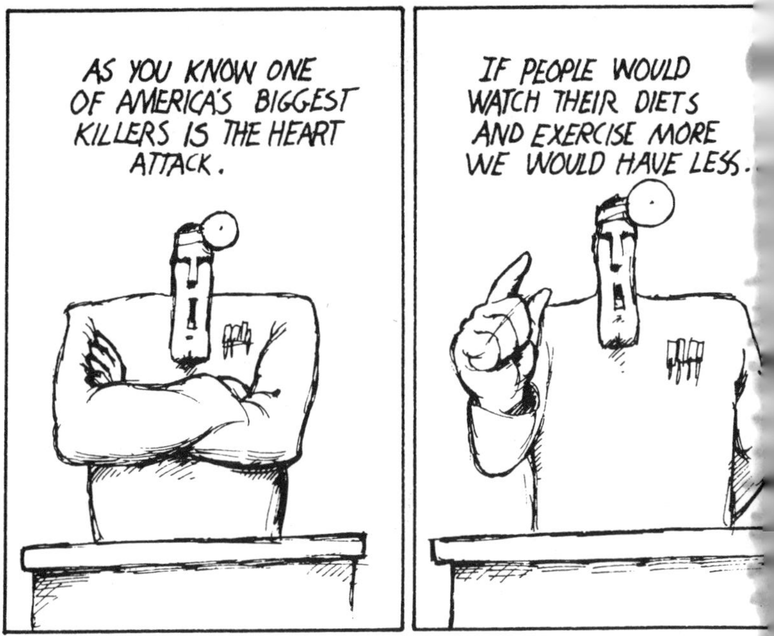
AS YOU KNOW ONE OF AMERICA'S BIGGEST KILLERS IS THE HEART ATTACK.
IF PEOPLE WOULD WATCH THEIR DIETS AND EXERCISE MORE WE WOULD HAVE LESS.

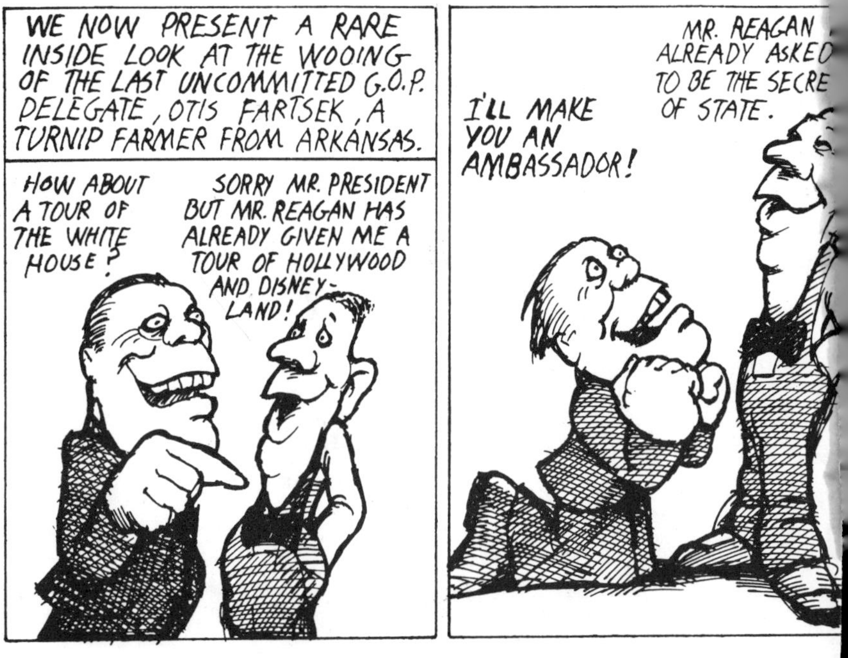
WE NOW PRESENT A RARE INSIDE LOOK AT THE WOOING OF THE LAST UNCOMMITTED G.O.P. DELEGATE, OTIS FARTSEK, A TURNIP FARMER FROM ARKANSAS.
HOW ABOUT A TOUR OF THE WHITE HOUSE?
SORRY MR. PRESIDENT BUT MR. REAGAN HAS ALREADY GIVEN ME A TOUR OF HOLLYWOOD AND DISNEY-LAND!
I'LL MAKE YOU AN AMBASSADOR!
MR. REAGAN
ALREADY ASKED
TO BE THE SECRE
OF STATE.

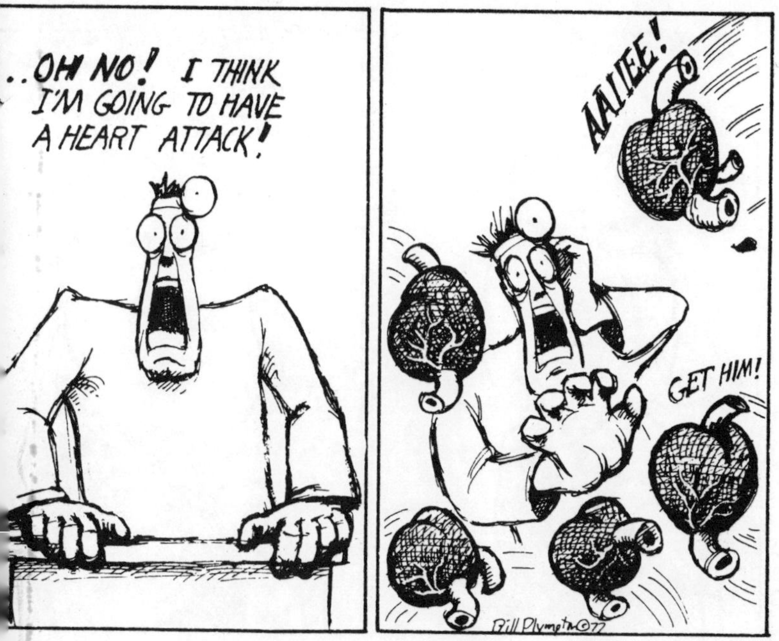
..OH NO! I THINK I'M GOING TO HAVE A HEART ATTACK!
AAIIEE!
GET HIM!
Bill Plympton©77

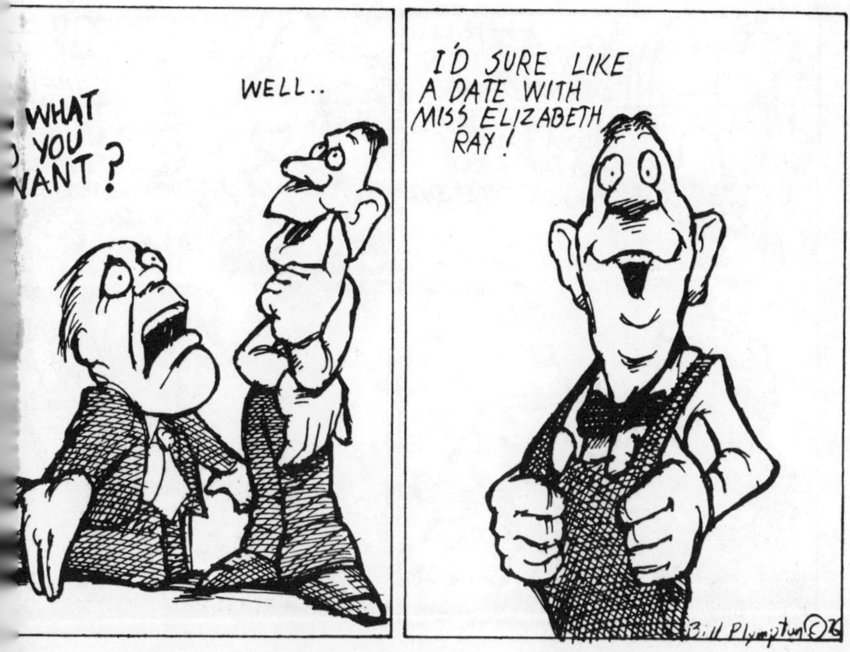
WHAT
YOU
VANT ?
WELL..
I'D SURE LIKE A DATE WITH MISS ELIZABETH RAY!
Bill Plympton©76

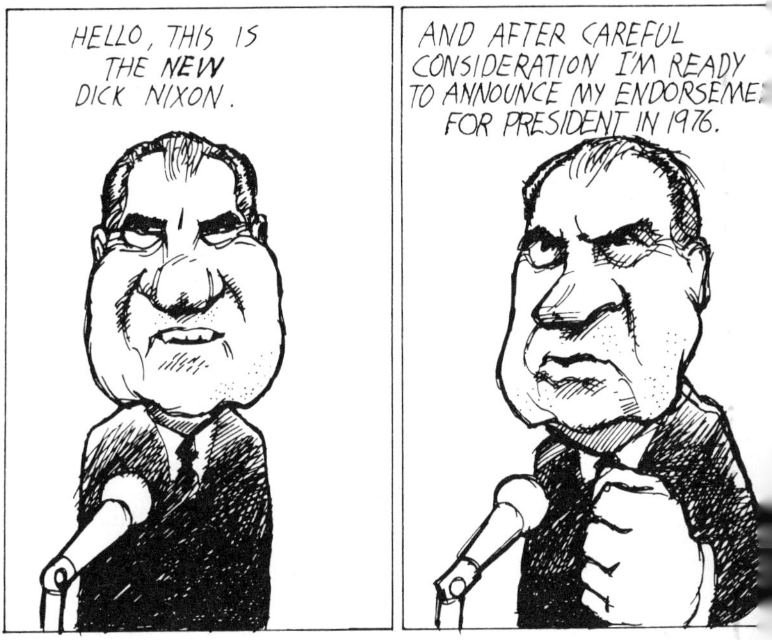
HELLO, THIS IS THE NEW DICK NIXON.
AND AFTER CAREFUL CONSIDERATION I'M READY TO ANNOUNCE MY ENDORSEME
FOR PRESIDENT IN 1976.

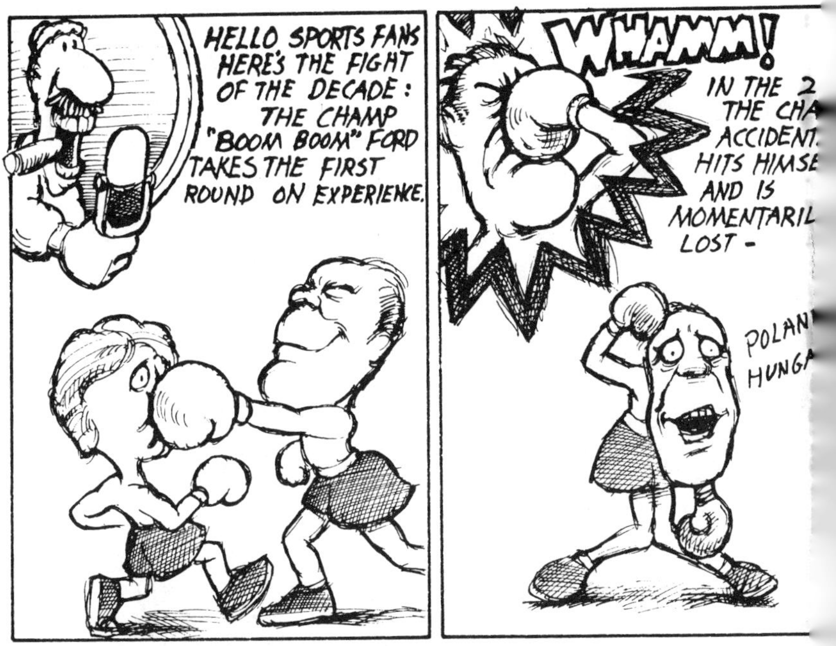
HELLO SPORTS FANS HERE'S THE FIGHT OF THE DECADE: THE CHAMP "BOOM BOOM" FORD TAKES THE FIRST ROUND ON EXPERIENCE.
WHAMM!
IN THE 2
THE CHA
ACCIDENT
HITS HIMSE
AND IS
MOMENTARIL
LOST -
POLAN
HUNGA

AND IT IS—

MMM....

Bill Plympton © 1976

IN THE THIRD ROUND BOTH "BOOM BOOM" FORD AND SMILIN" JIMMY CARTER HIT HARD, BUT CARTER LOOKS A LITTLE FASTER ON HIS FEET.

SO THAT'S THE FIGHT! NOW REMEMBER—AS OFFICIAL JUDGES YOU MUST HAND IN YOUR DECISION BY NOV. 2.

Bill Plympton © 76

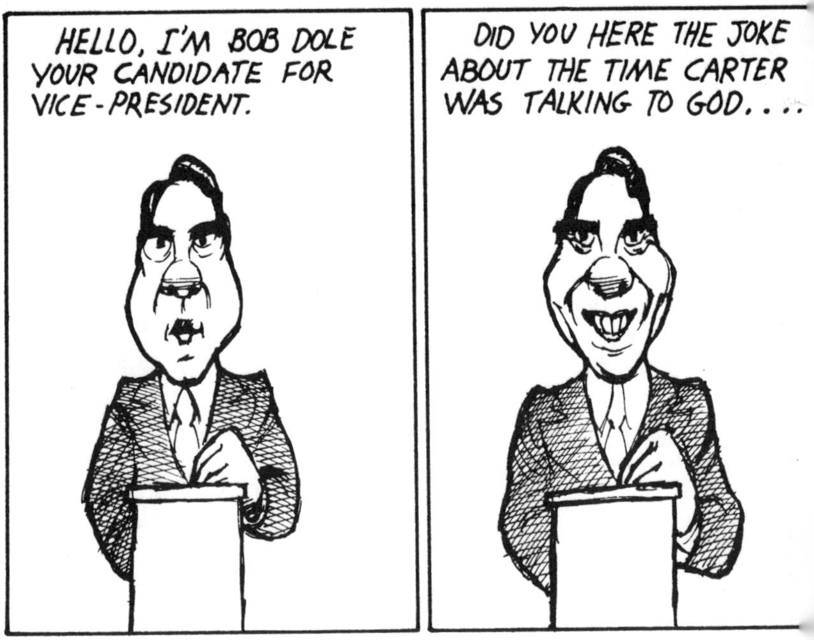
HELLO, I'M BOB DOLE YOUR CANDIDATE FOR VICE-PRESIDENT.
DID YOU HERE THE JOKE ABOUT THE TIME CARTER WAS TALKING TO GOD....

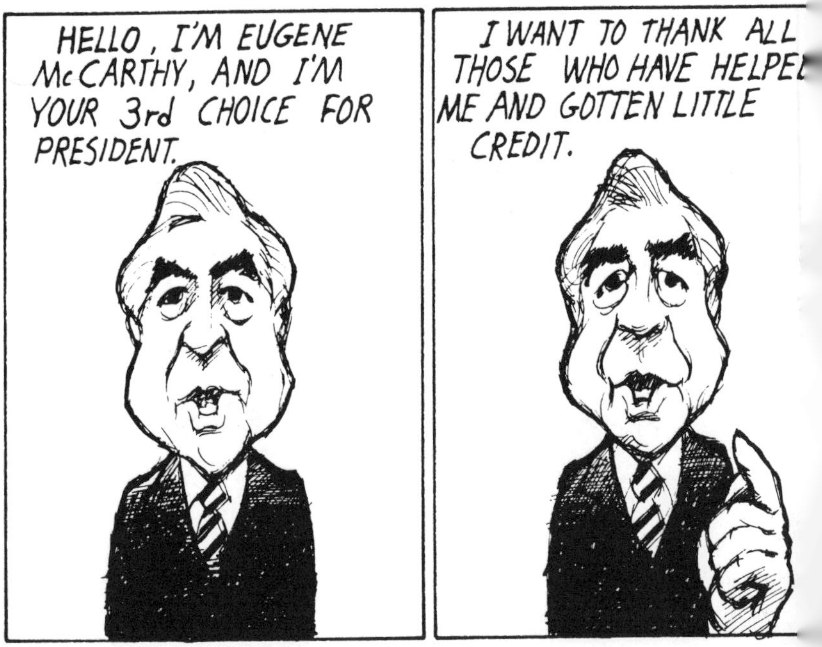
HELLO, I'M EUGENE McCARTHY, AND I'M YOUR 3rd CHOICE FOR PRESIDENT.
I WANT TO THANK ALL THOSE WHO HAVE HELPE
ME AND GOTTEN LITTLE CREDIT.

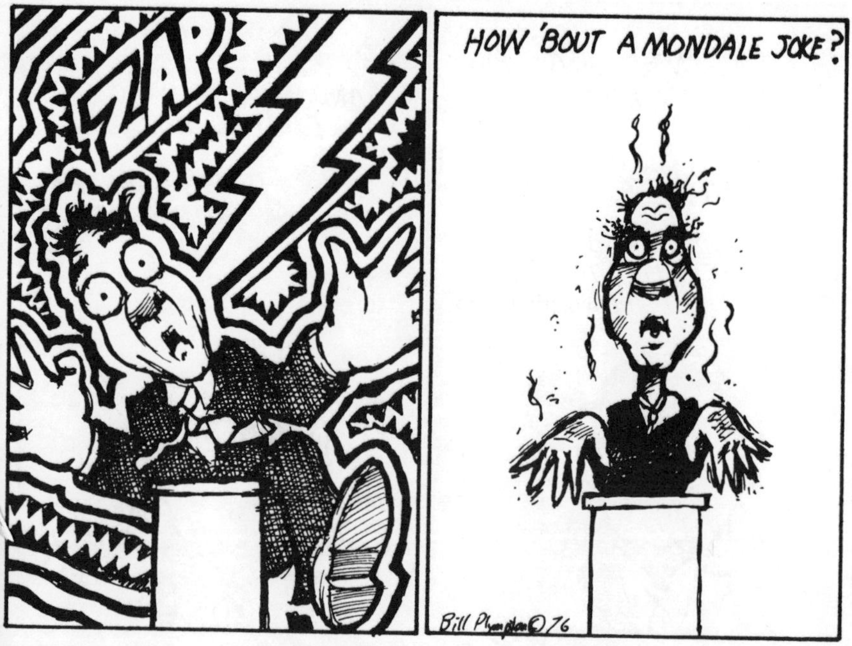
ZAP
HOW 'BOUT A MONDALE JOKE?
Bill Plympton © 76

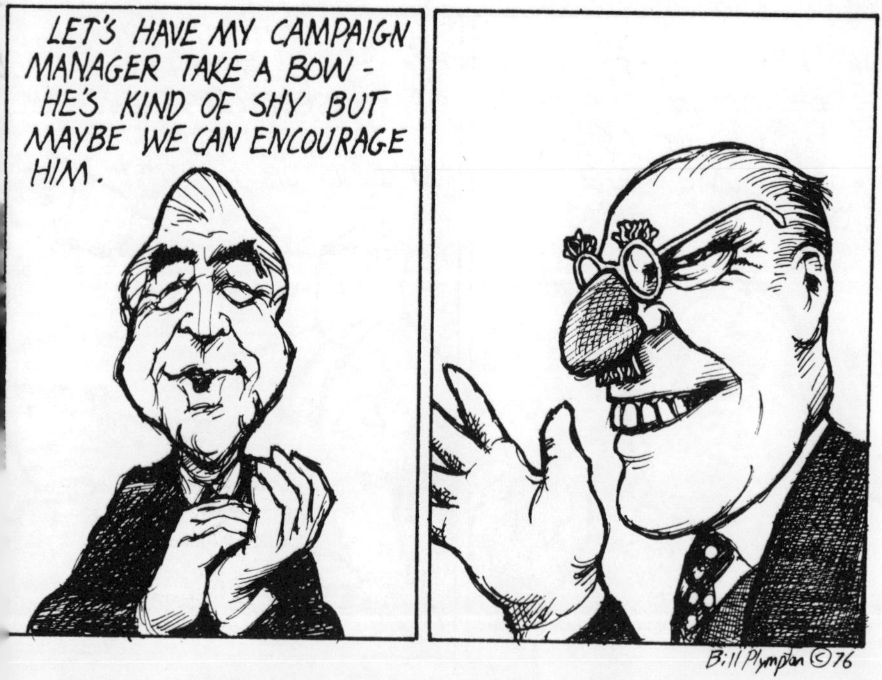
LET'S HAVE MY CAMPAIGN MANAGER TAKE A BOW - HE'S KIND OF SHY BUT MAYBE WE CAN ENCOURAGE HIM.
Bill Plympton © 76

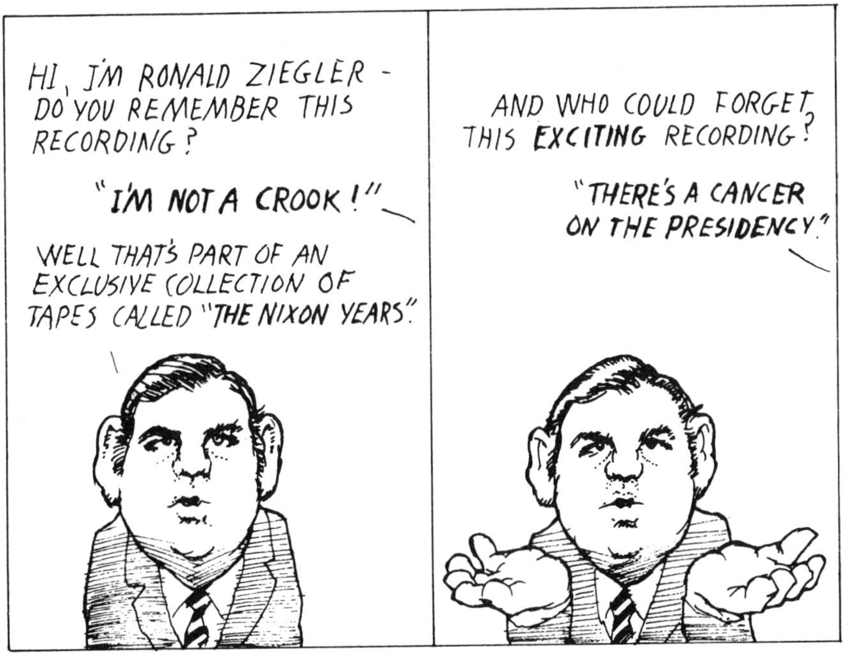
HI, I'M RONALD ZIEGLER - DO YOU REMEMBER THIS RECORDING?
"I'M NOT A CROOK!"
WELL THAT'S PART OF AN EXCLUSIVE COLLECTION OF TAPES CALLED "THE NIXON YEARS".
AND WHO COULD FORGET THIS EXCITING RECORDING?
"THERE'S A CANCER ON THE PRESIDENCY."

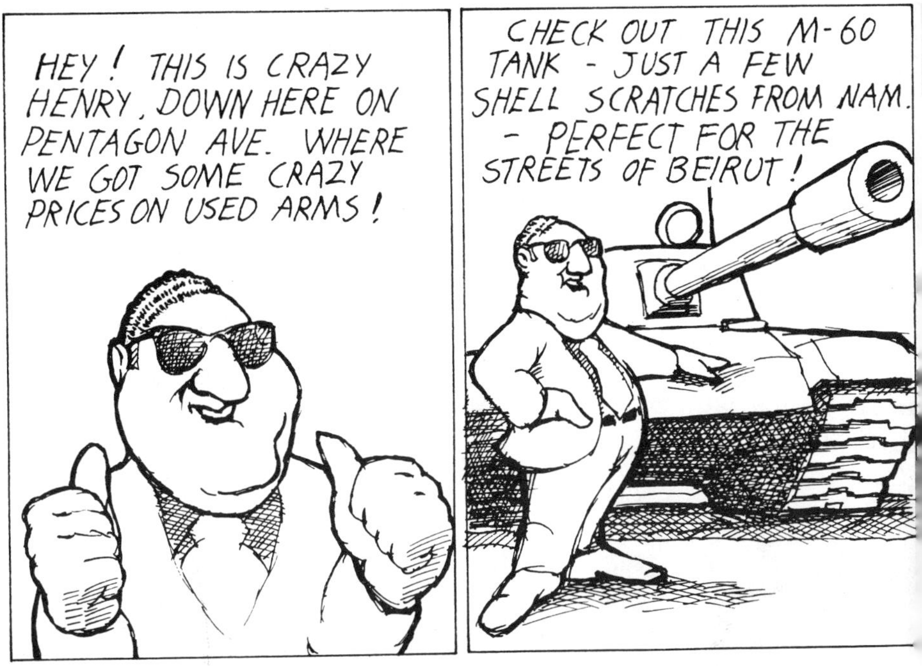
HEY! THIS IS CRAZY HENRY, DOWN HERE ON PENTAGON AVE. WHERE WE GOT SOME CRAZY PRICES ON USED ARMS!
CHECK OUT THIS M-60 TANK - JUST A FEW SHELL SCRATCHES FROM NAM. - PERFECT FOR THE STREETS OF BEIRUT!

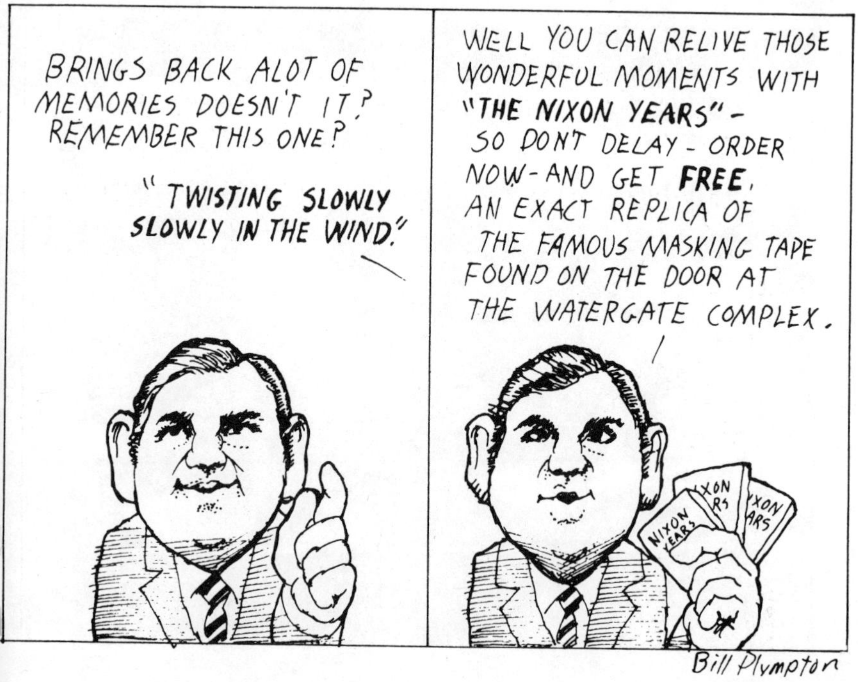
BRINGS BACK ALOT OF MEMORIES DOESN'T IT? REMEMBER THIS ONE?
"TWISTING SLOWLY SLOWLY IN THE WIND."
WELL YOU CAN RELIVE THOSE WONDERFUL MOMENTS WITH **"THE NIXON YEARS"** - SO DON'T DELAY - ORDER NOW - AND GET **FREE**, AN EXACT REPLICA OF THE FAMOUS MASKING TAPE FOUND ON THE DOOR AT THE WATERGATE COMPLEX.
NIXON YEARS
Bill Plympton

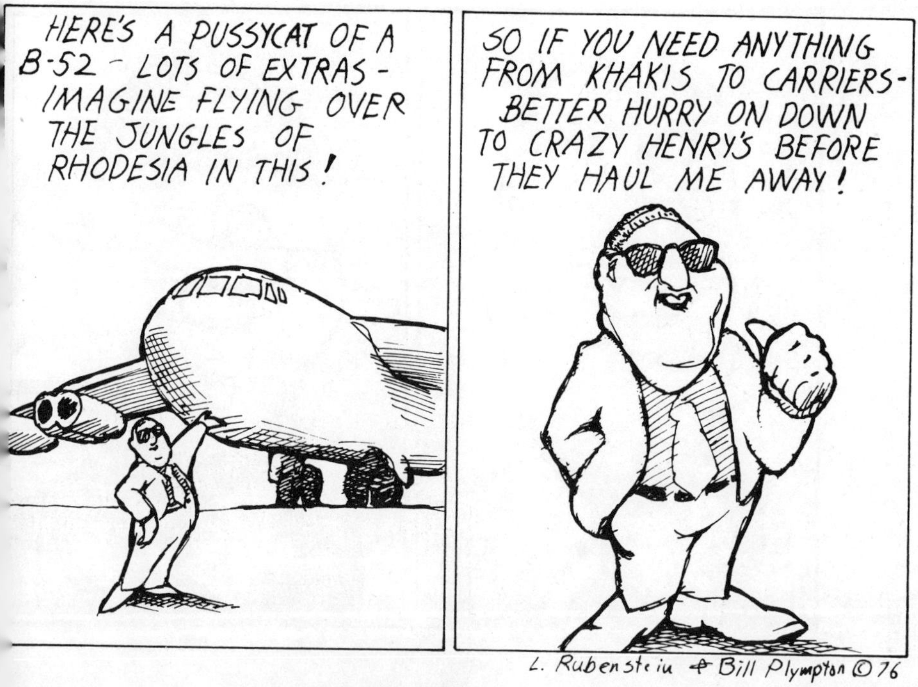
HERE'S A PUSSYCAT OF A B-52 - LOTS OF EXTRAS - IMAGINE FLYING OVER THE JUNGLES OF RHODESIA IN THIS!
SO IF YOU NEED ANYTHING FROM KHAKIS TO CARRIERS - BETTER HURRY ON DOWN TO CRAZY HENRY'S BEFORE THEY HAUL ME AWAY!
L. Rubenstein & Bill Plympton © 76

WE'VE HAD SOME WONDERFUL ADVENTURES TOGETHER - CHINA, THE SOVIET UNION AFRICA, CHILE, THE MIDDLE EAST, AND WHO COULD FORGET VIETNAM!
BUT AS WITH ALL GOOD THINGS, THEY MUST COME TO AN END SOMETIME

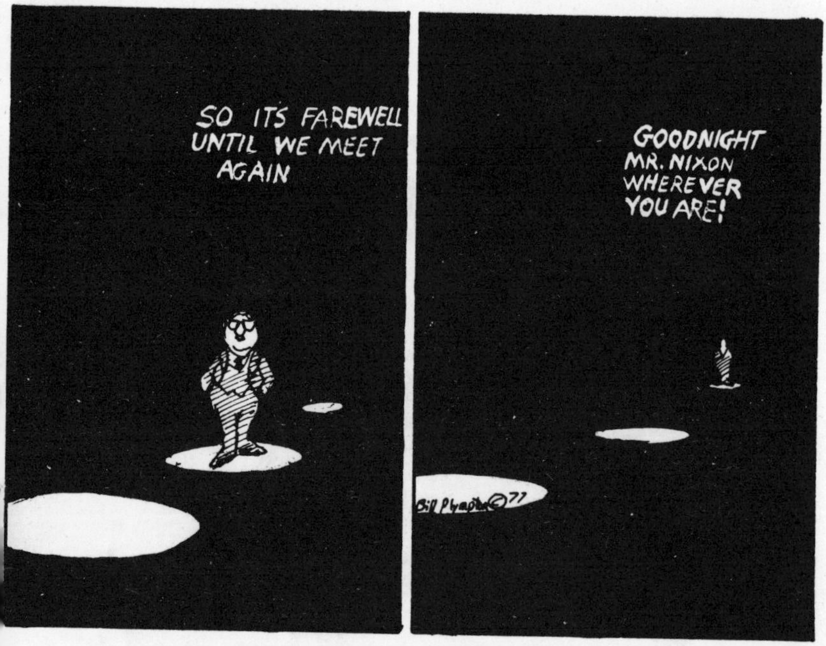
SO ITS FAREWELL UNTIL WE MEET AGAIN
GOODNIGHT MR. NIXON WHEREVER YOU ARE!
Bill Plympton ©77

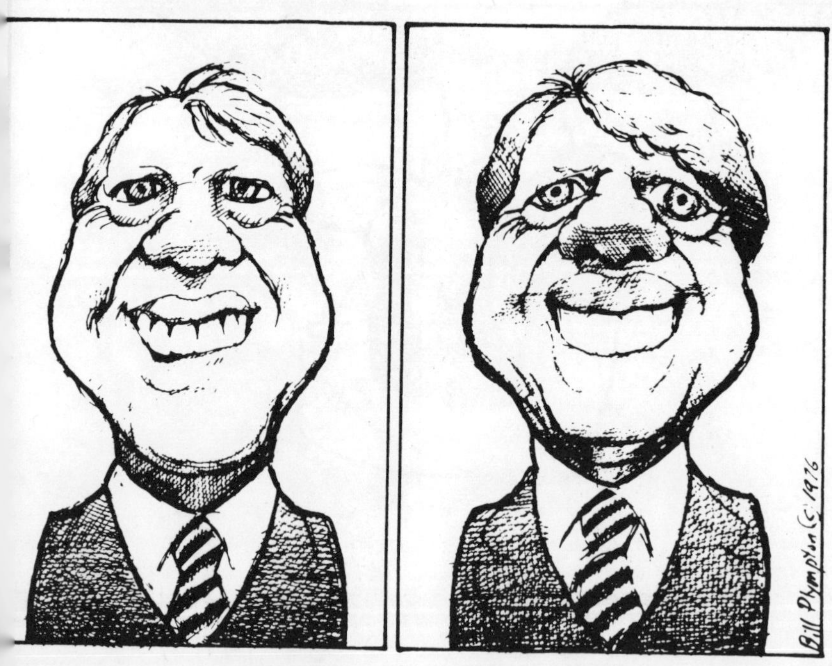
Bill Plympton (c) 1976

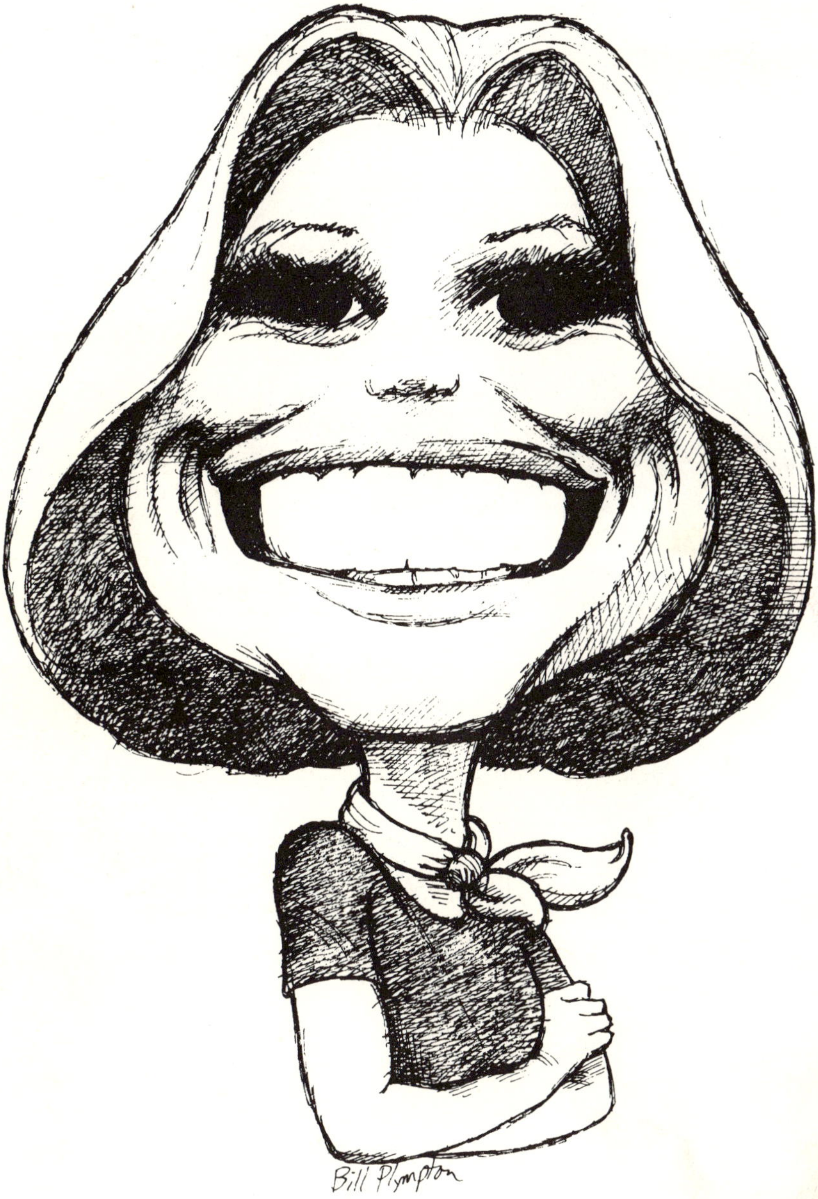
Bill Plympton

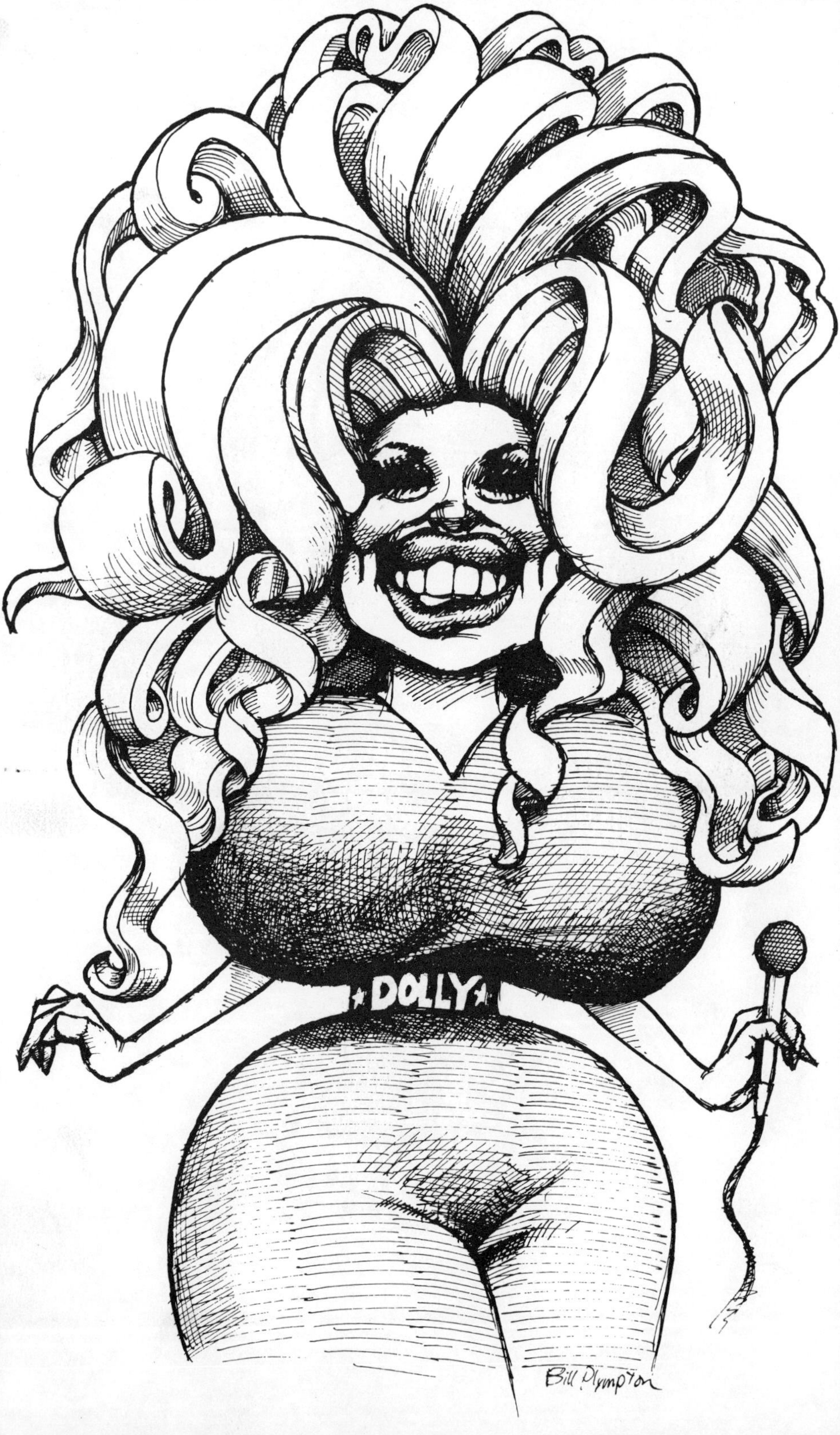
DOLLY
Bill Plympton

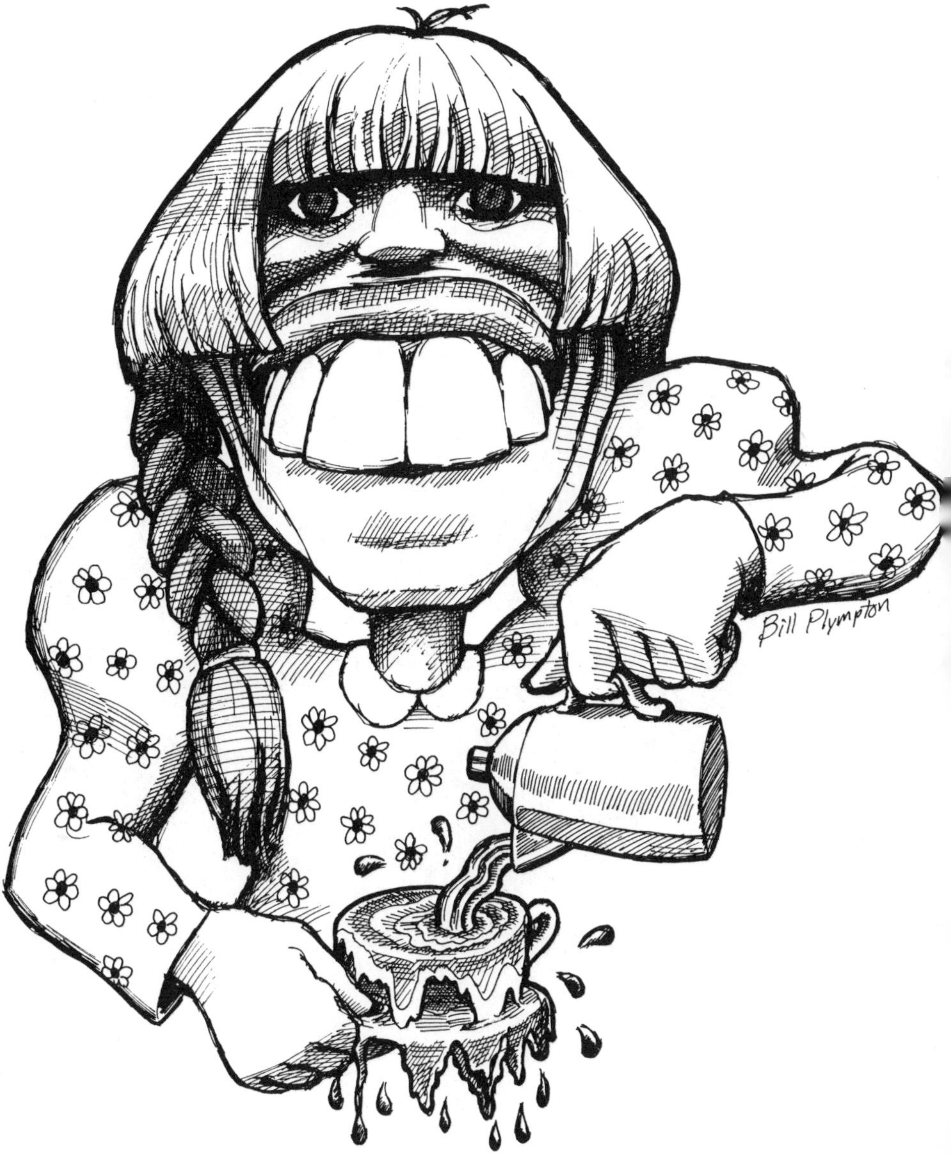
Bill Plympton

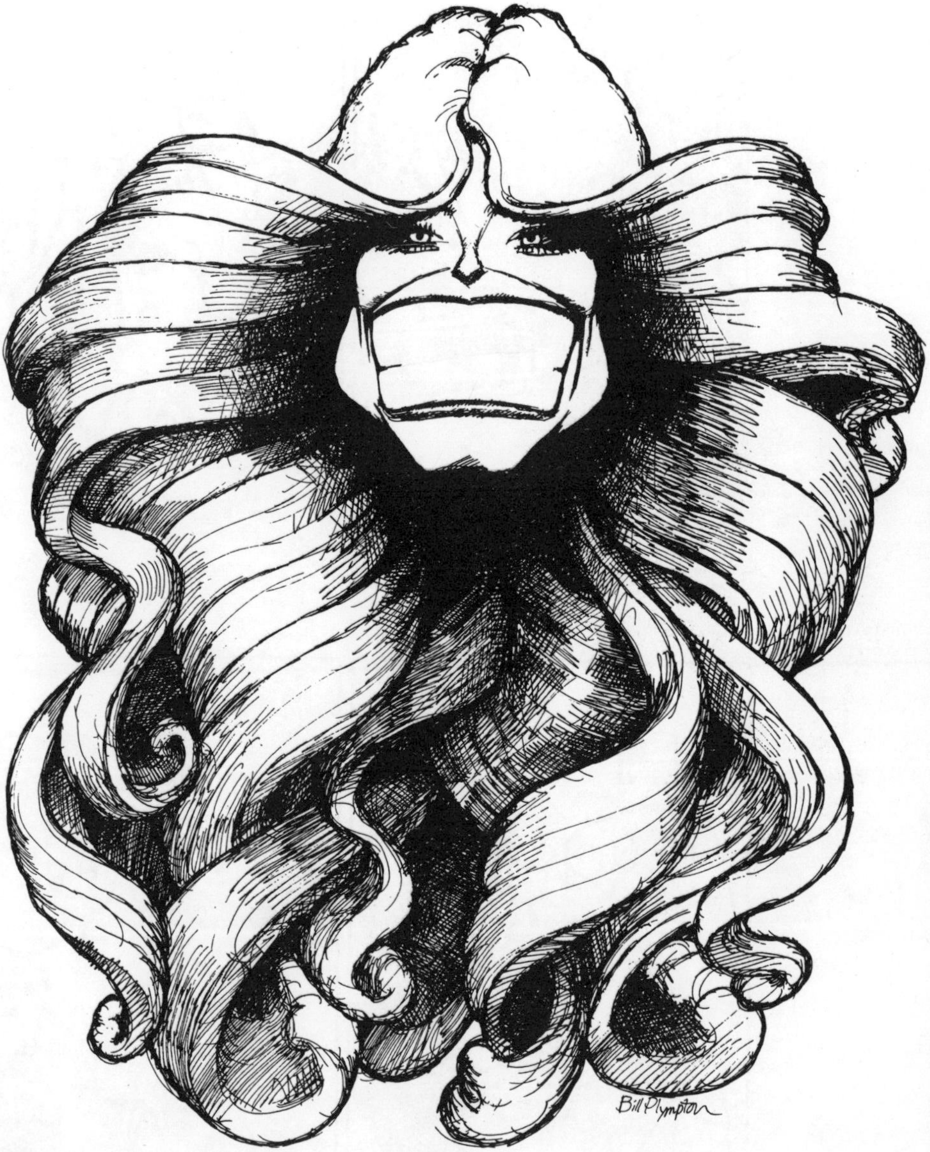
Bill Plympton

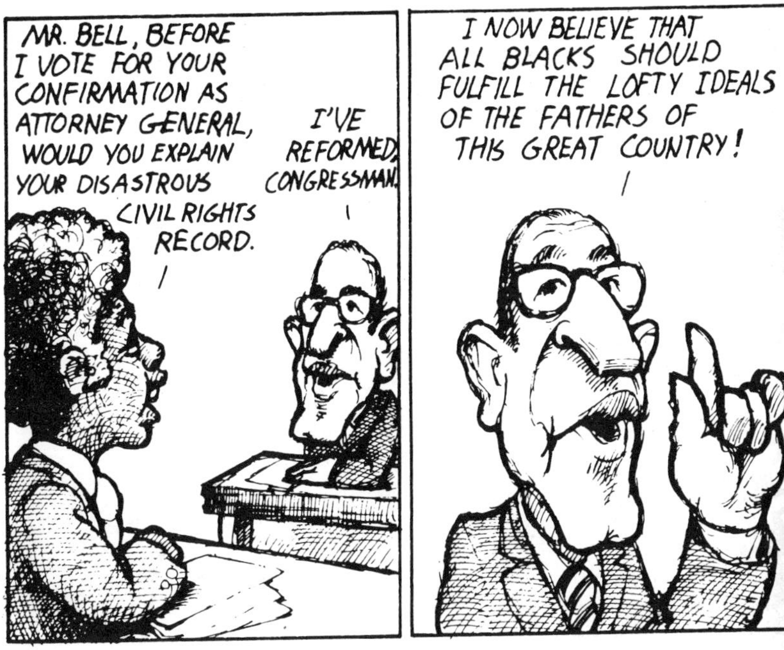
MR. BELL, BEFORE I VOTE FOR YOUR CONFIRMATION AS ATTORNEY GENERAL, WOULD YOU EXPLAIN YOUR DISASTROUS CIVIL RIGHTS RECORD.
I'VE REFORMED, CONGRESSMAN!
I NOW BELIEVE THAT ALL BLACKS SHOULD FULFILL THE LOFTY IDEALS OF THE FATHERS OF THIS GREAT COUNTRY!

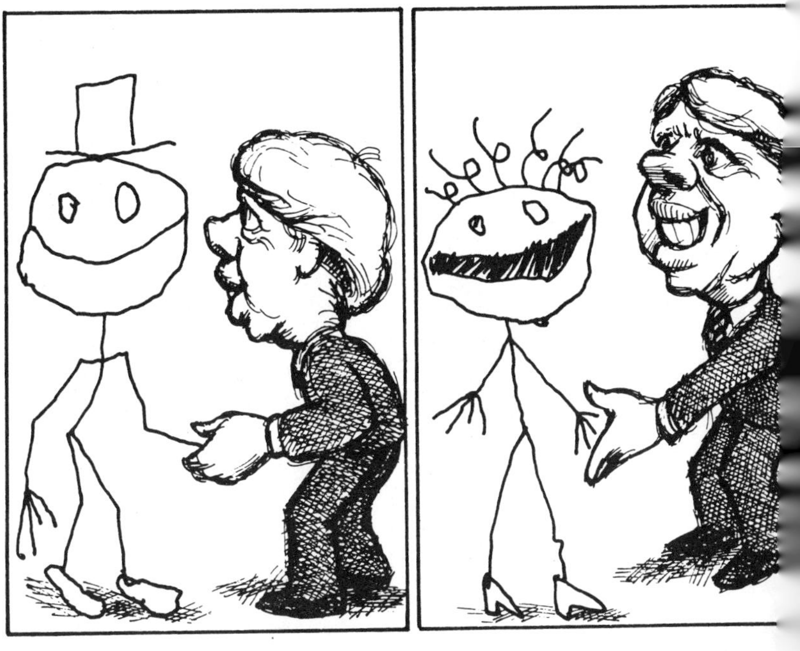

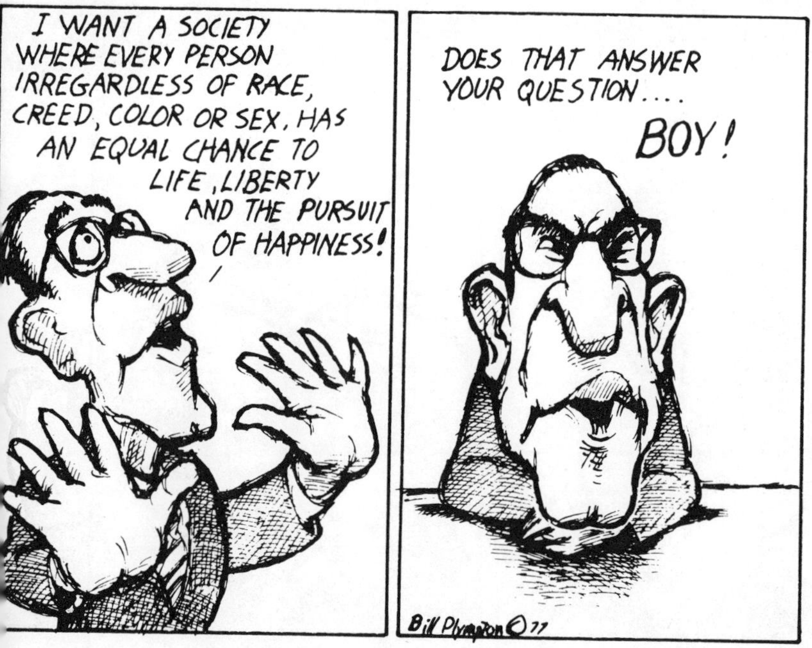
I WANT A SOCIETY WHERE EVERY PERSON IRREGARDLESS OF RACE, CREED, COLOR OR SEX, HAS AN EQUAL CHANCE TO LIFE, LIBERTY AND THE PURSUIT OF HAPPINESS!
DOES THAT ANSWER YOUR QUESTION....
BOY!
Bill Plympton©77

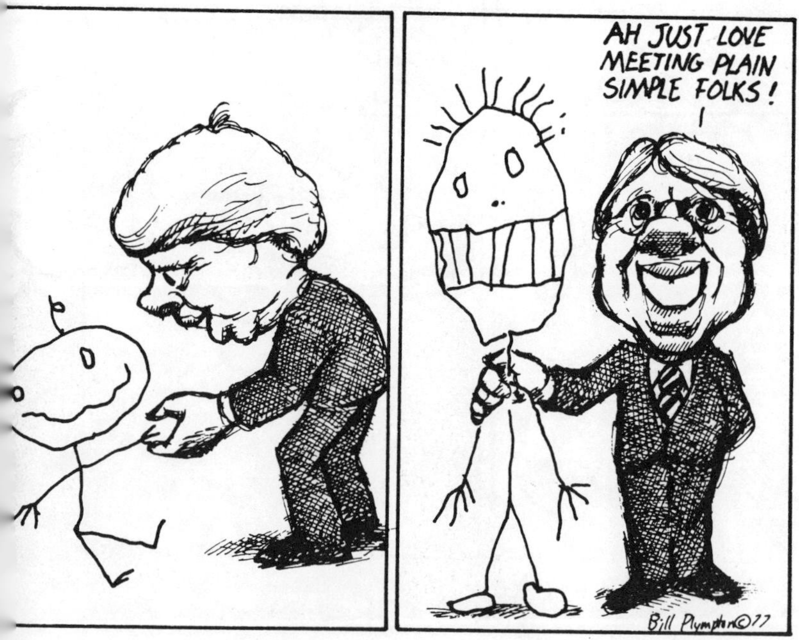
AH JUST LOVE MEETING PLAIN SIMPLE FOLKS!
Bill Plympton©77

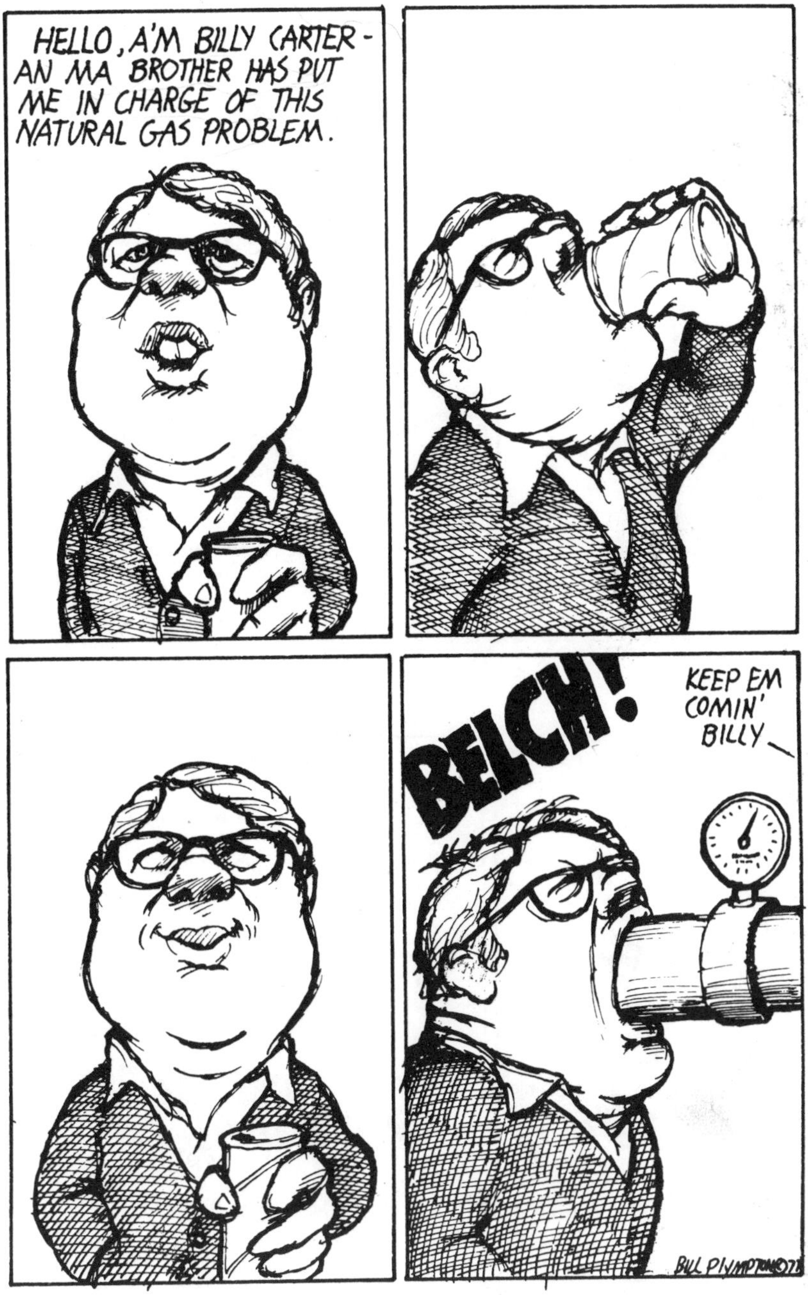
HELLO, A'M BILLY CARTER - AN MA BROTHER HAS PUT ME IN CHARGE OF THIS NATURAL GAS PROBLEM.
BELCH!
KEEP EM COMIN' BILLY
BILL PLYMPTON©77

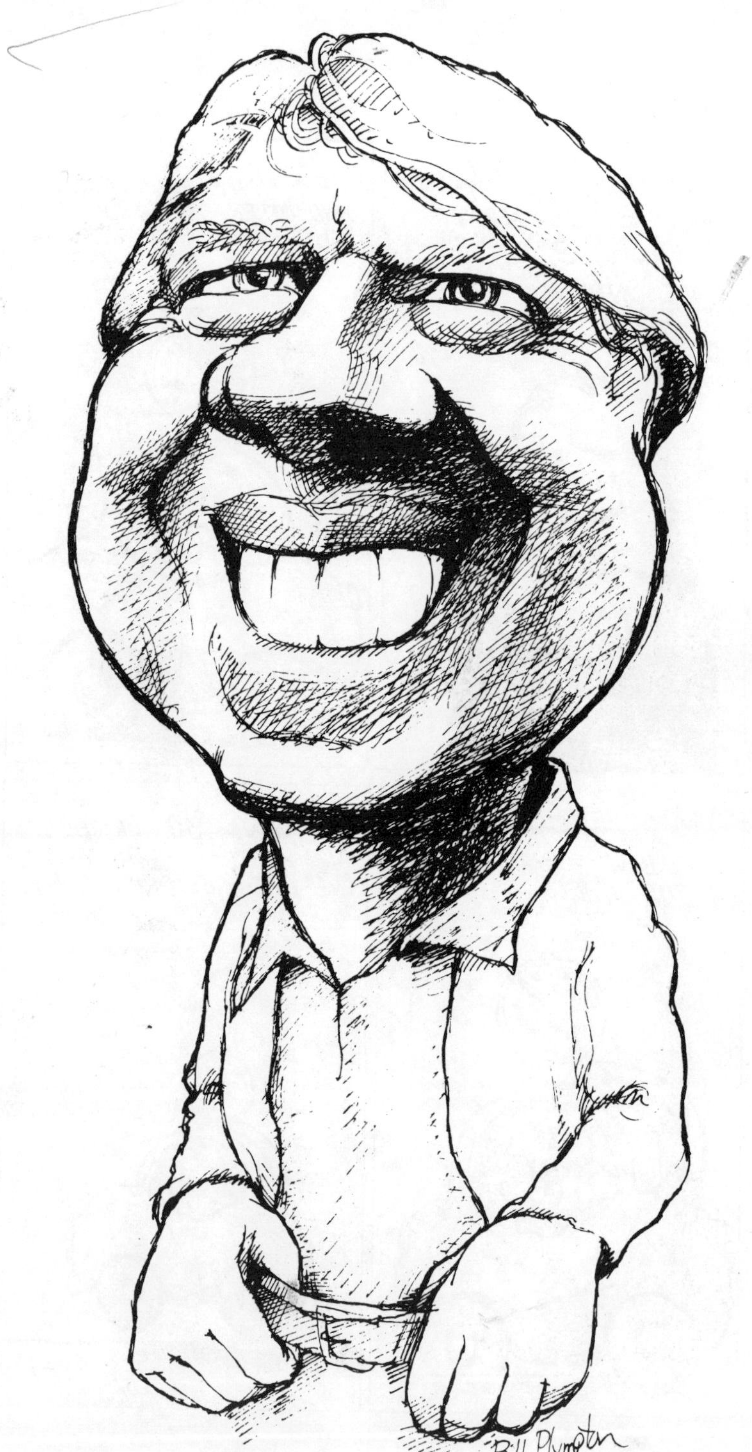
Bill Plympton

THIS IS ENERGY CHIEF JAMES SCHLESINGER WITH OUR ANSWER TO THE OIL SHORTAGE — THE *"INTERNAL FRUSTRATION ENGINE"*!

STEP 1 THE DRIVER, CAUGHT IN TRAFFIC, HIGH COSTS AND OTHER DAILY FRUSTRATIONS, RAISES THE CABIN PRESSURE.

STEP 2 THE HOT AIR PASSES THRU THE TURBINE - TURNING THE WHEEL

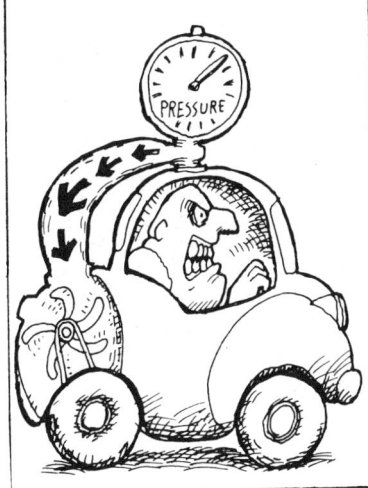

LEAVING THE DRIVER, AND AMERICA, WITH MILES-OF *GAS-FREE* DRIVING!

Bill Plympton

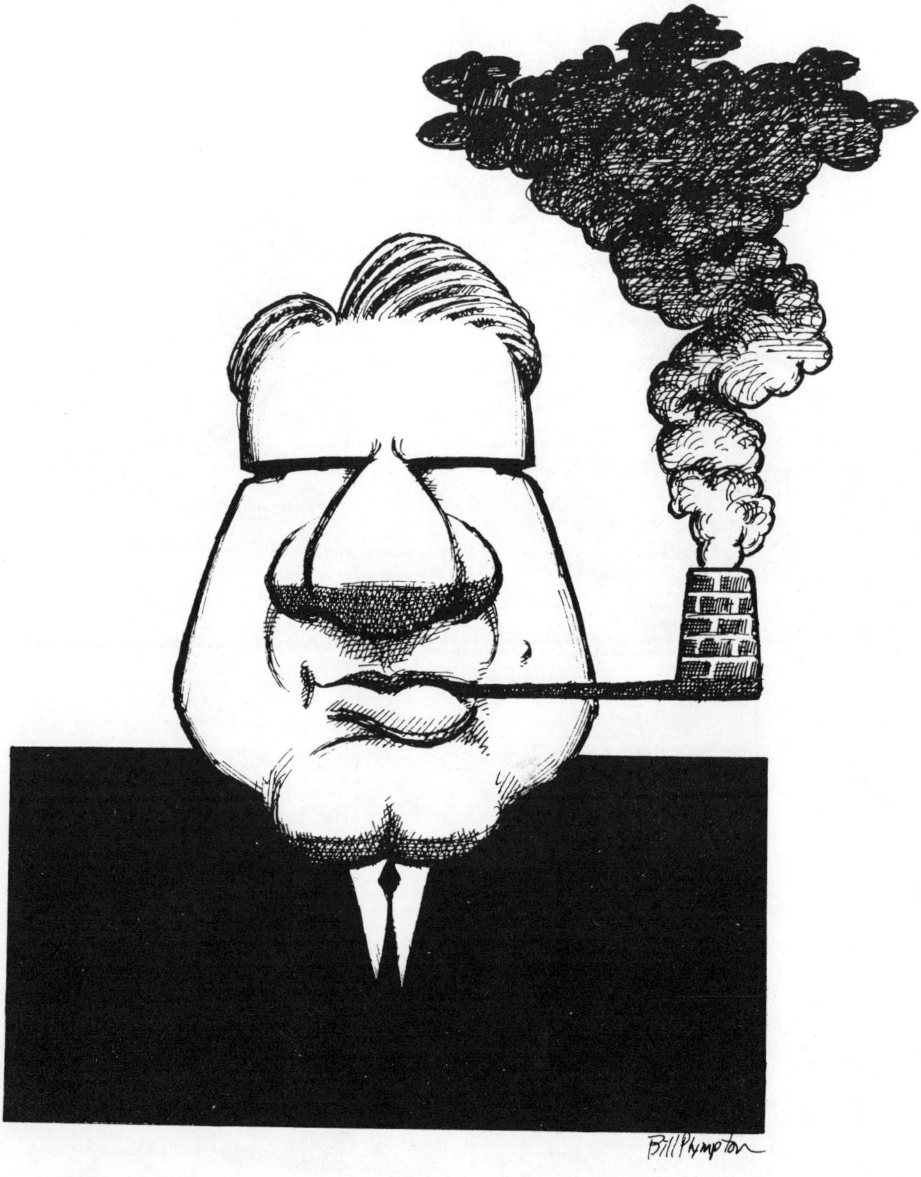
Bill Plympton

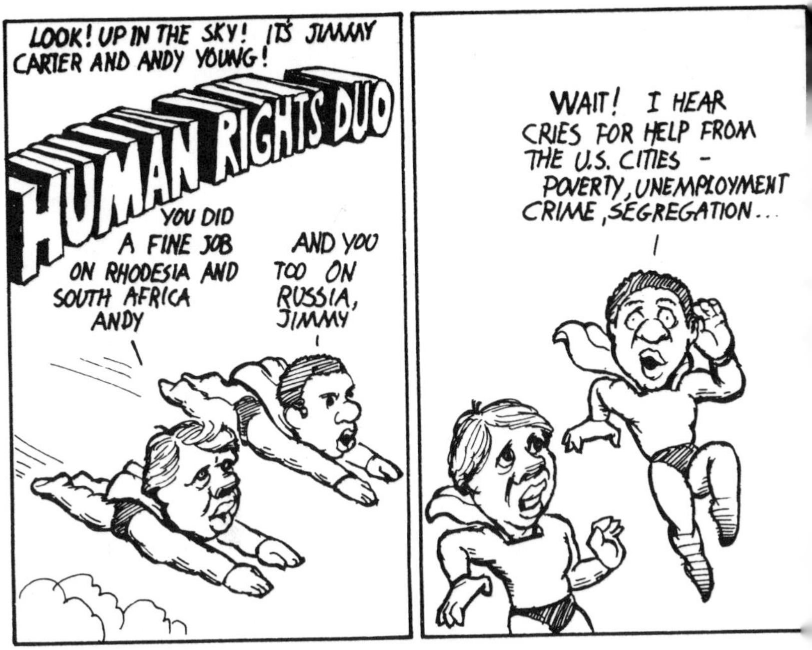
LOOK! UP IN THE SKY! IT'S JIMMY CARTER AND ANDY YOUNG!
HUMAN RIGHTS DUO
YOU DID A FINE JOB ON RHODESIA AND SOUTH AFRICA ANDY
AND YOU TOO ON RUSSIA, JIMMY
WAIT! I HEAR CRIES FOR HELP FROM THE U.S. CITIES - POVERTY, UNEMPLOYMENT CRIME, SEGREGATION...

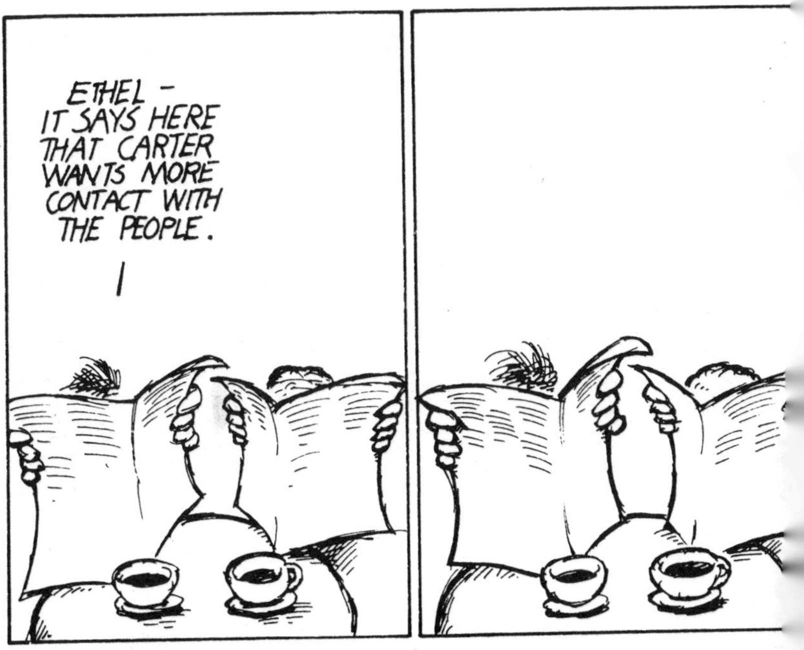
ETHEL - IT SAYS HERE THAT CARTER WANTS MORE CONTACT WITH THE PEOPLE.

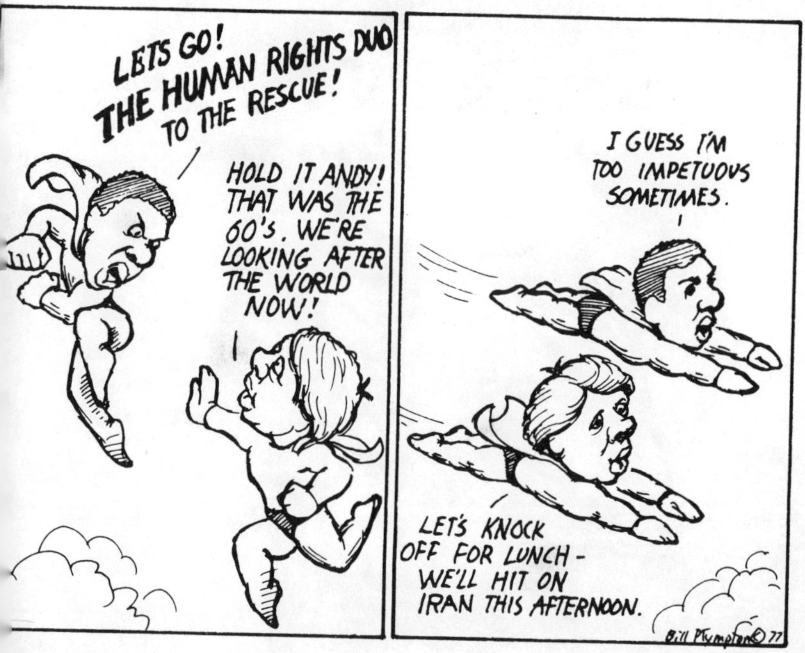
LETS GO! THE HUMAN RIGHTS DUO TO THE RESCUE!
HOLD IT ANDY! THAT WAS THE 60'S. WE'RE LOOKING AFTER THE WORLD NOW!
I GUESS I'M TOO IMPETUOUS SOMETIMES.
LET'S KNOCK OFF FOR LUNCH - WE'LL HIT ON IRAN THIS AFTERNOON.
Bill Plympton © 77

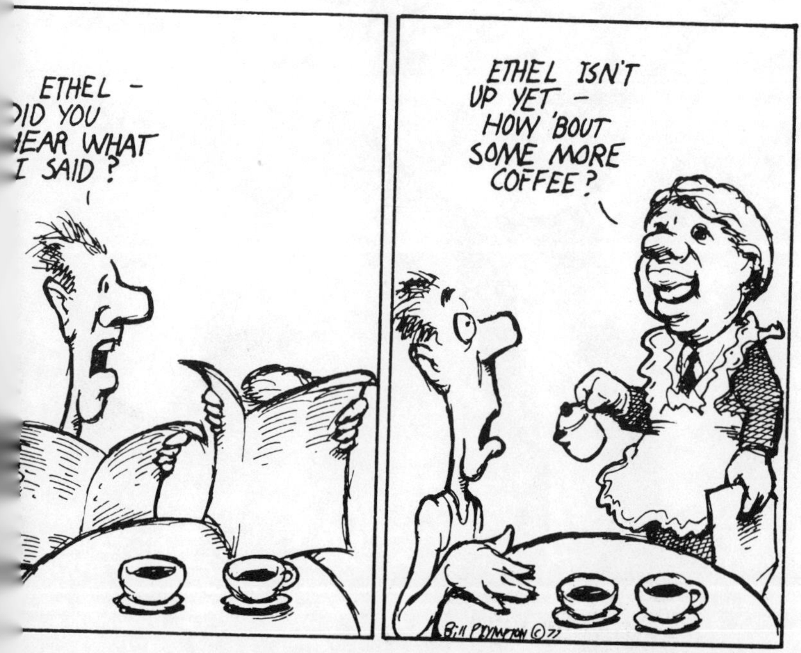
ETHEL - DID YOU HEAR WHAT I SAID ?
ETHEL ISN'T UP YET - HOW 'BOUT SOME MORE COFFEE?
Bill Plympton © 77

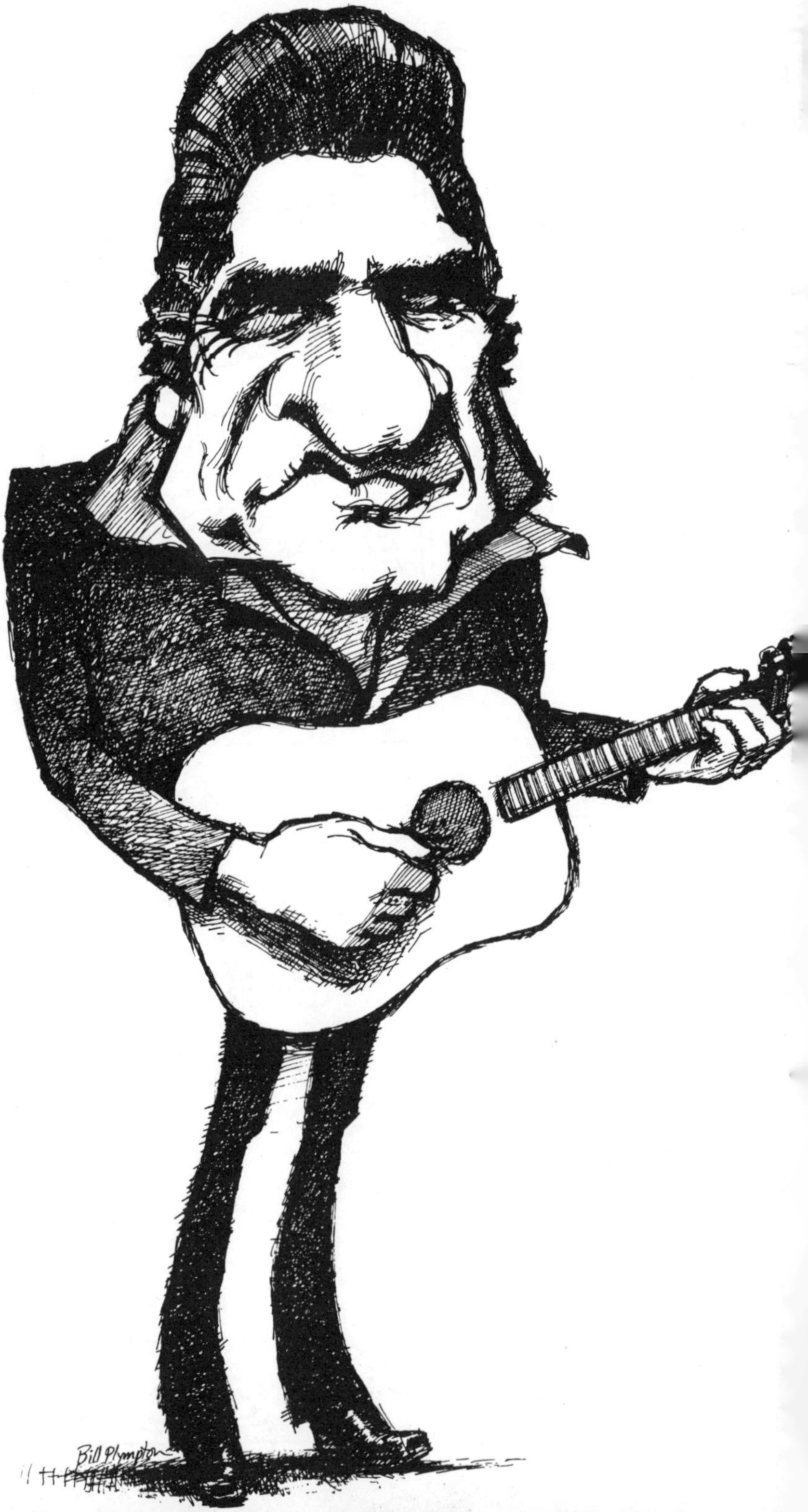
Bill Plympton

AND AS USUAL THE PUBLIC WILL ALL WANT LARGE TEETH TO BECOME GLAMOROUS TOO!

BUT AS WITH ALL CRAZES IT WILL SOON FADE AND END UP IN THE ATTIC WITH ALL THE OTHERS.

VIOLENCE IS FINE IN FILMS —

BUT VIOLENCE IN REAL LIFE GETS YOU ARRESTED.

YET SEX IS FINE IN REAL LIFE —

BUT SEX IN FILMS GETS YOU ARRESTED !

Bill Phampion © 77

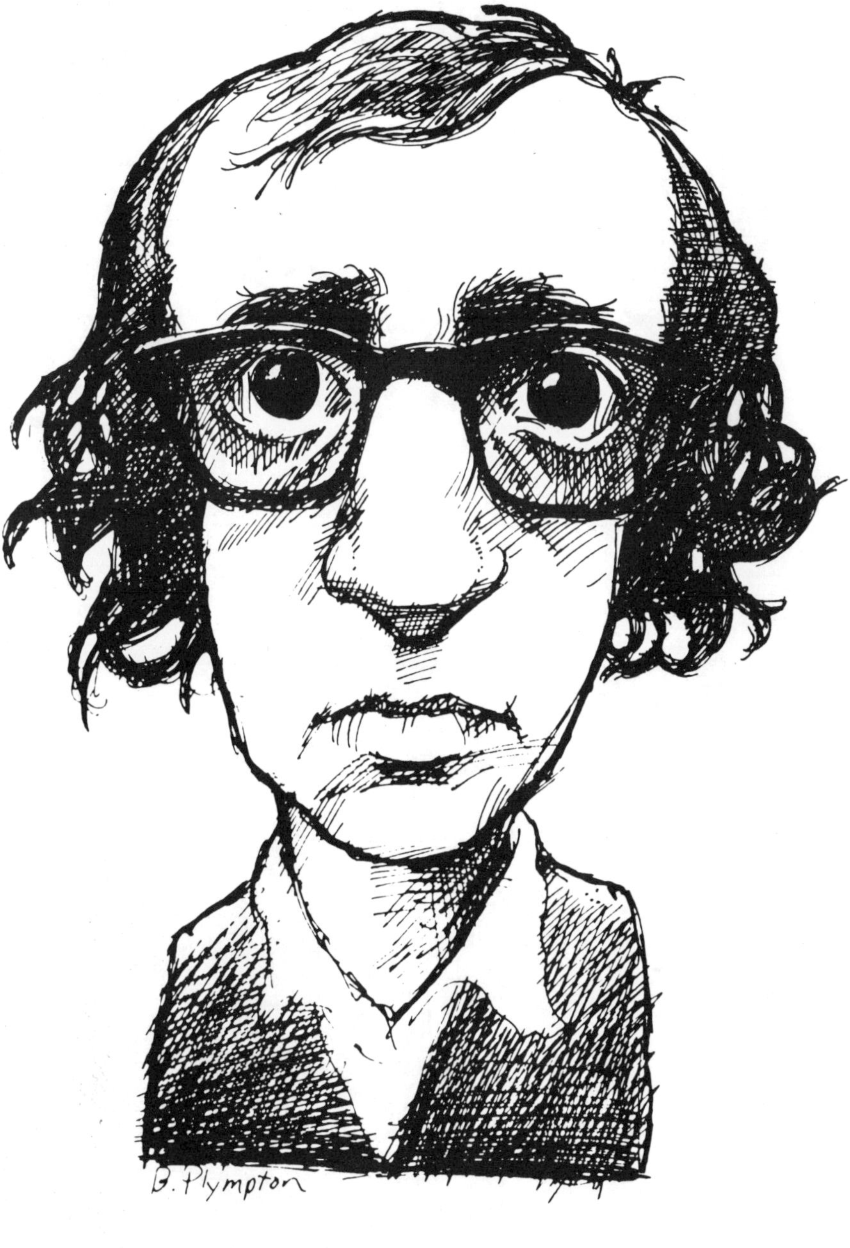
B. Plympton

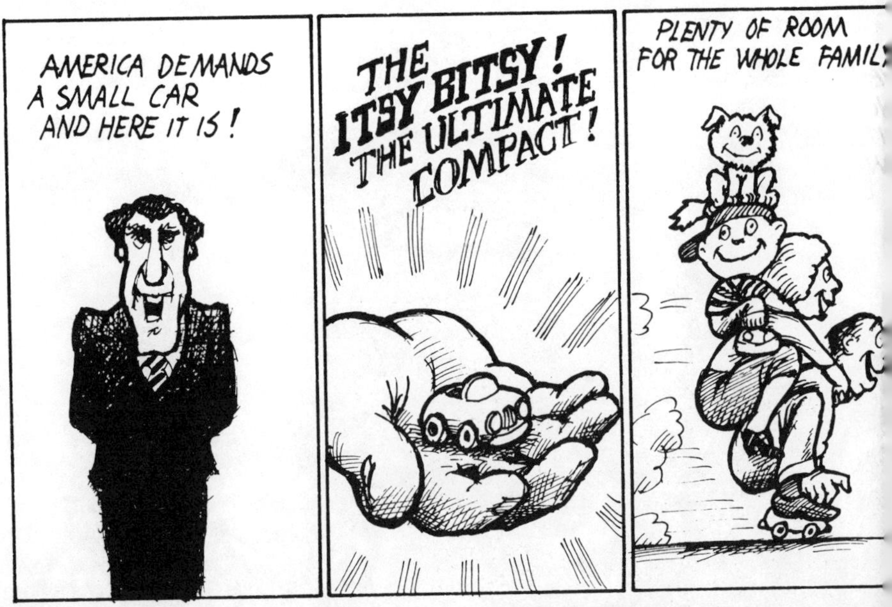
AMERICA DEMANDS A SMALL CAR AND HERE IT IS!
THE ITSY BITSY! THE ULTIMATE COMPACT!
PLENTY OF ROOM FOR THE WHOLE FAMIL

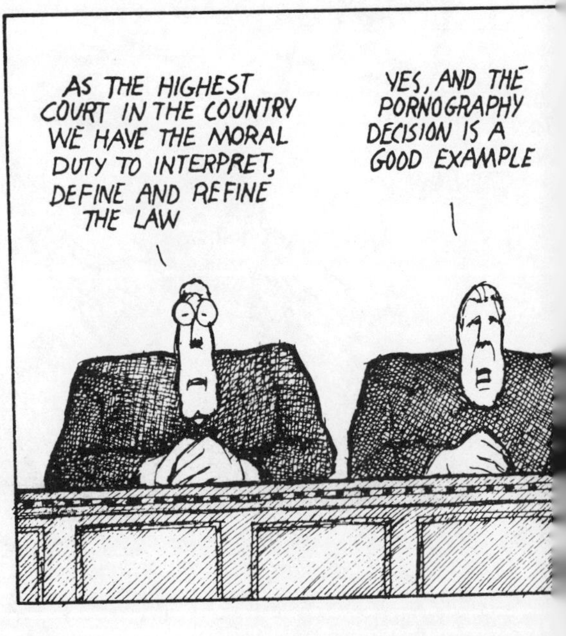
AS THE HIGHEST COURT IN THE COUNTRY WE HAVE THE MORAL DUTY TO INTERPRET, DEFINE AND REFINE THE LAW
YES, AND THE PORNOGRAPHY DECISION IS A GOOD EXAMPLE

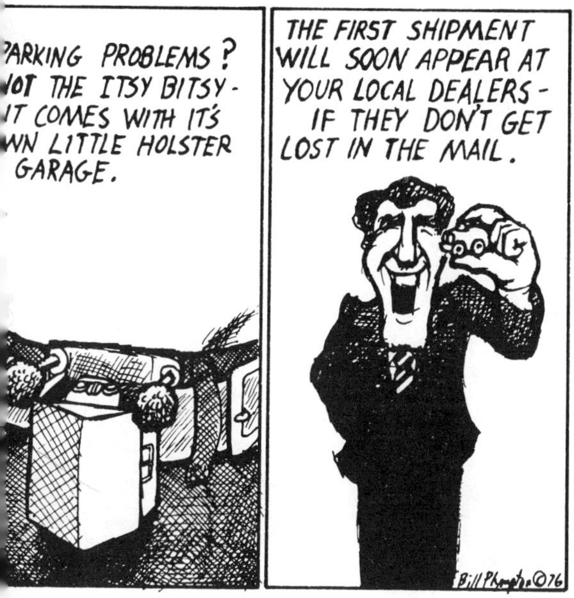
ARKING PROBLEMS? NOT THE ITSY BITSY - IT COMES WITH IT'S WN LITTLE HOLSTER GARAGE.
THE FIRST SHIPMENT WILL SOON APPEAR AT YOUR LOCAL DEALERS - IF THEY DON'T GET LOST IN THE MAIL.
Bill Plympton ©76

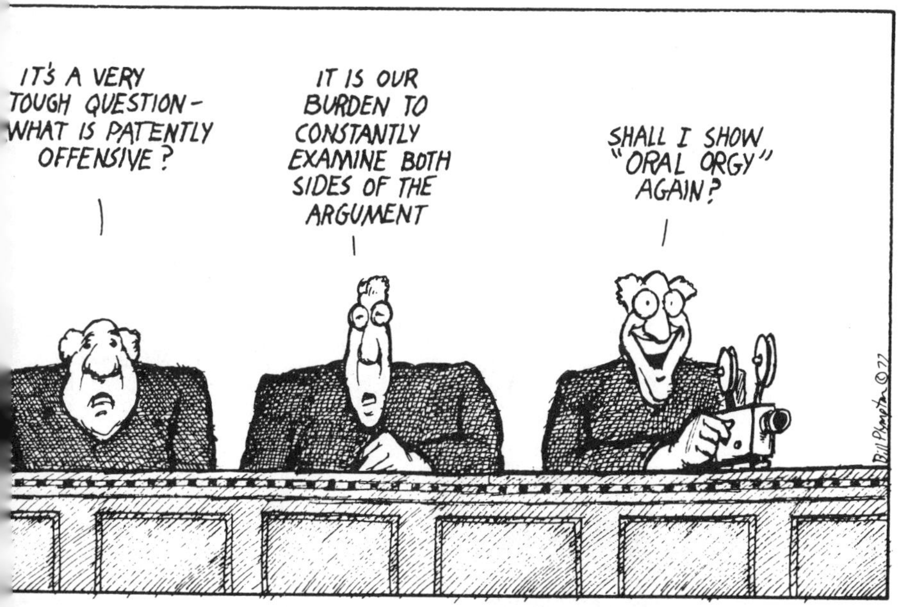
IT'S A VERY TOUGH QUESTION - WHAT IS PATENTLY OFFENSIVE?
IT IS OUR BURDEN TO CONSTANTLY EXAMINE BOTH SIDES OF THE ARGUMENT
SHALL I SHOW "ORAL ORGY" AGAIN?
Bill Plympton ©77

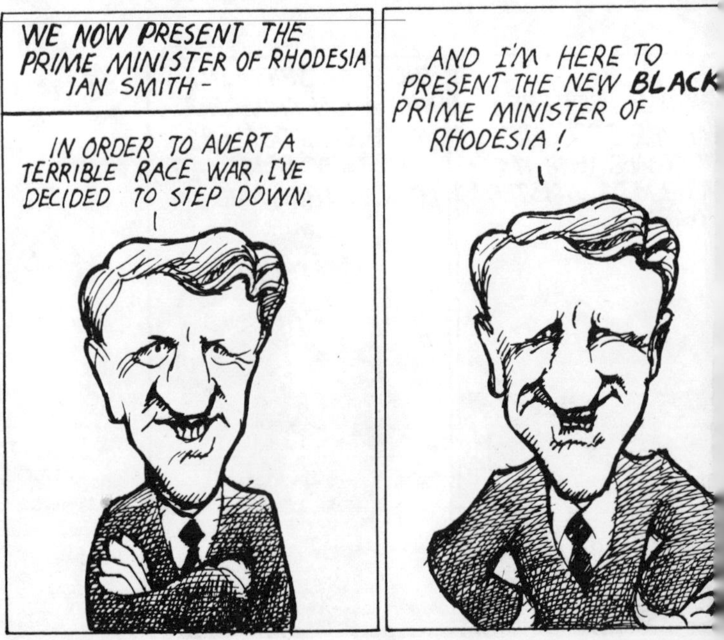
WE NOW PRESENT THE PRIME MINISTER OF RHODESIA IAN SMITH -
IN ORDER TO AVERT A TERRIBLE RACE WAR, I'VE DECIDED TO STEP DOWN.
AND I'M HERE TO PRESENT THE NEW BLACK PRIME MINISTER OF RHODESIA!

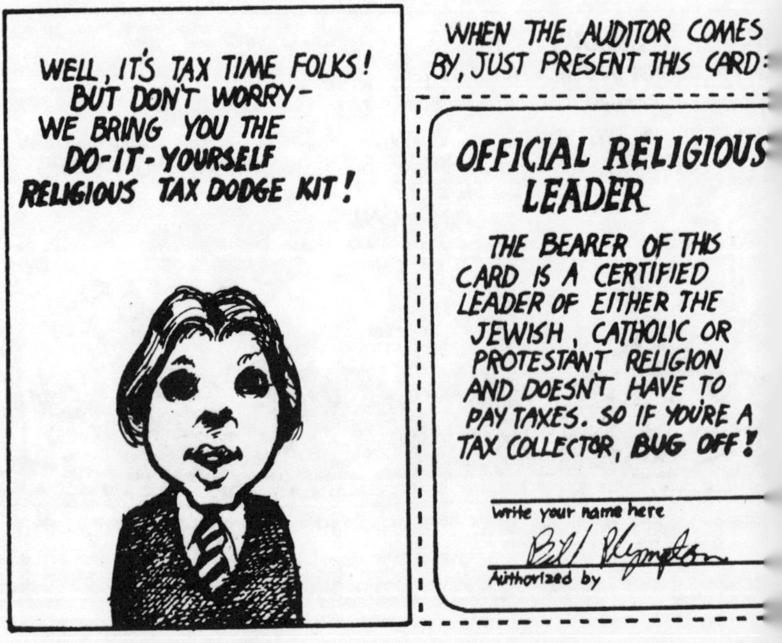
WELL, IT'S TAX TIME FOLKS! BUT DON'T WORRY - WE BRING YOU THE DO-IT-YOURSELF RELIGIOUS TAX DODGE KIT!
WHEN THE AUDITOR COMES BY, JUST PRESENT THIS CARD:
OFFICIAL RELIGIOUS LEADER
THE BEARER OF THIS CARD IS A CERTIFIED LEADER OF EITHER THE JEWISH, CATHOLIC OR PROTESTANT RELIGION AND DOESN'T HAVE TO PAY TAXES. SO IF YOU'RE A TAX COLLECTOR, BUG OFF!
write your name here
Authorized by

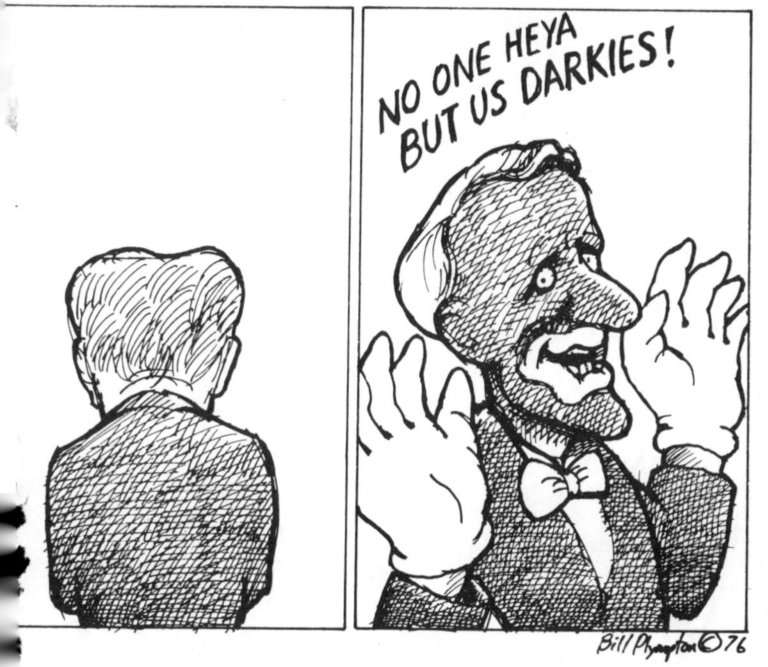
NO ONE HEYA
BUT US DARKIES!
Bill Plympton©76

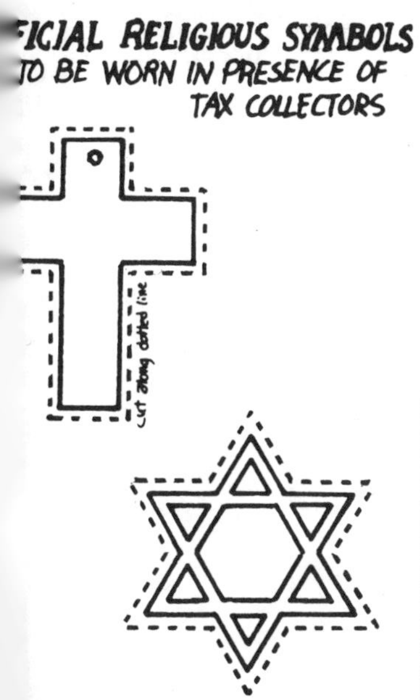
FICIAL RELIGIOUS SYMBOLS
TO BE WORN IN PRESENCE OF
TAX COLLECTORS
cut along dotted line

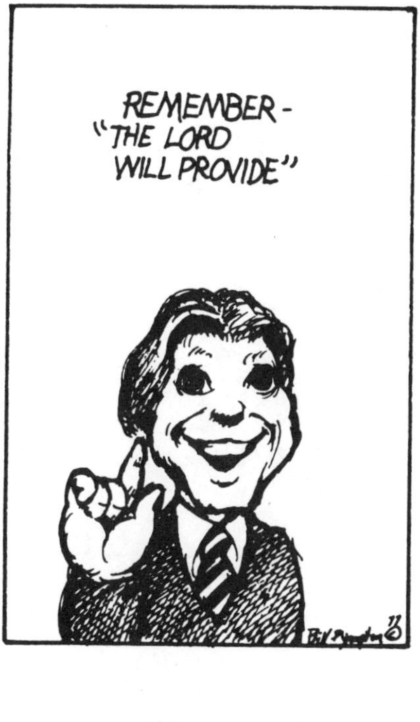
REMEMBER -
"THE LORD
WILL PROVIDE"

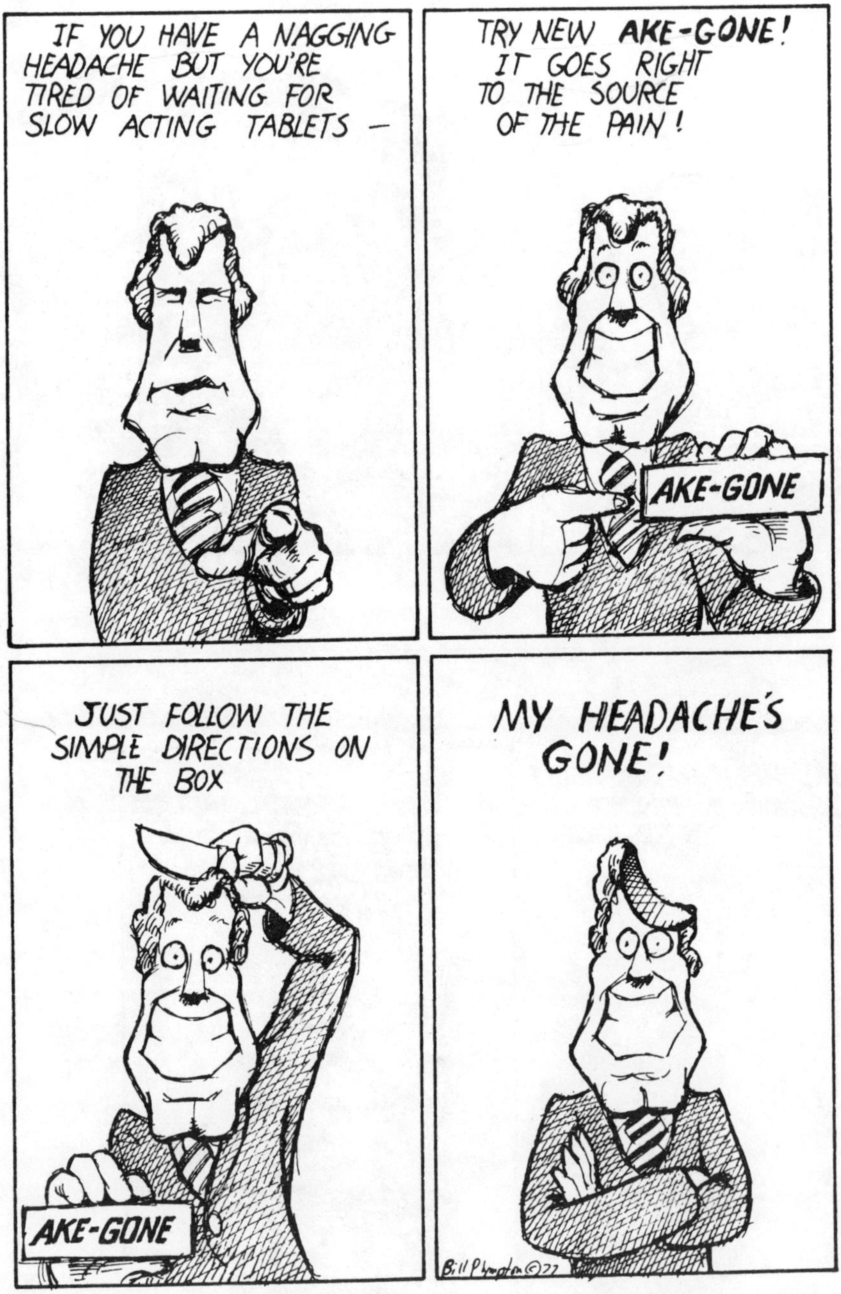
IF YOU HAVE A NAGGING HEADACHE BUT YOU'RE TIRED OF WAITING FOR SLOW ACTING TABLETS —
TRY NEW AKE-GONE! IT GOES RIGHT TO THE SOURCE OF THE PAIN!
AKE-GONE
JUST FOLLOW THE SIMPLE DIRECTIONS ON THE BOX
AKE-GONE
MY HEADACHE'S GONE!
Bill Plympton ©77

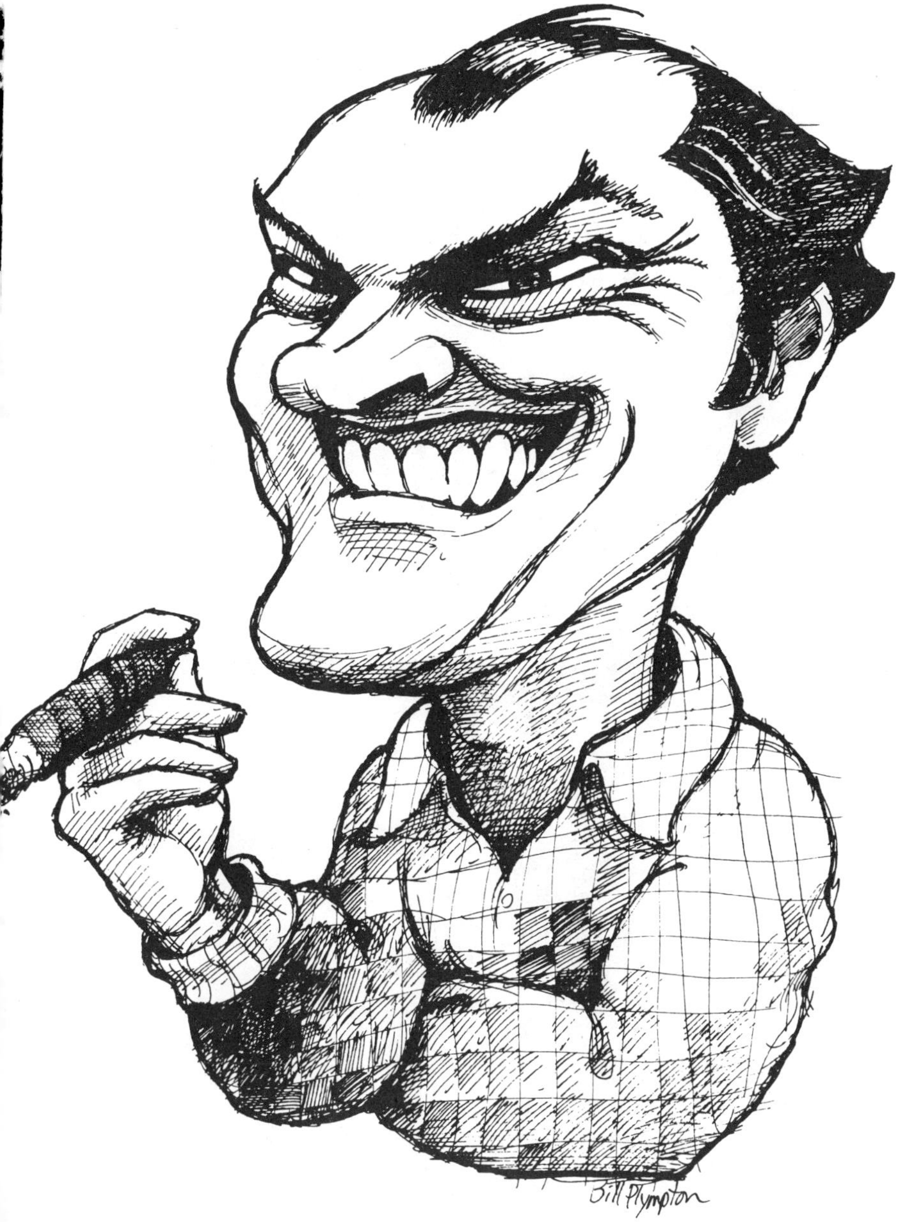
Bill Plympton

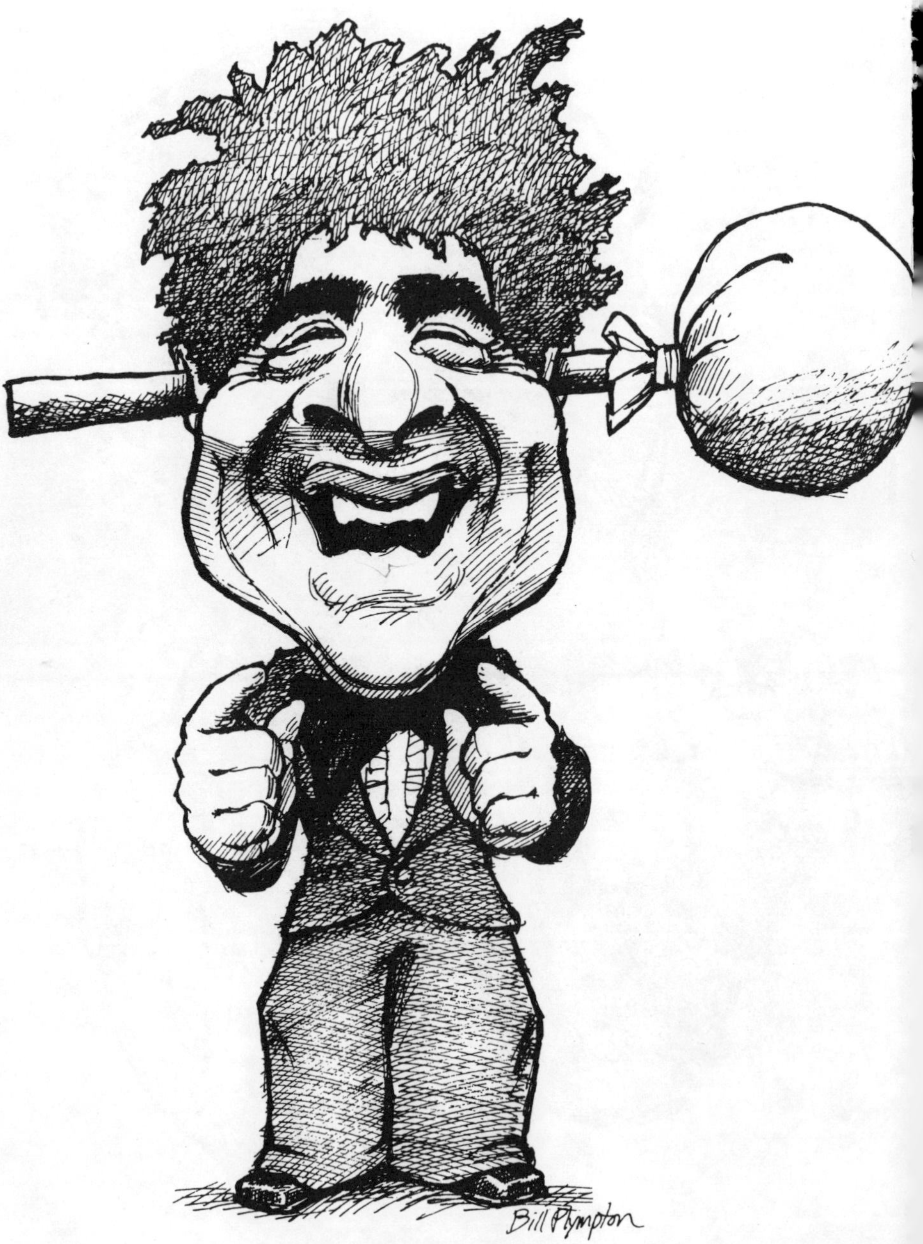
Bill Plympton

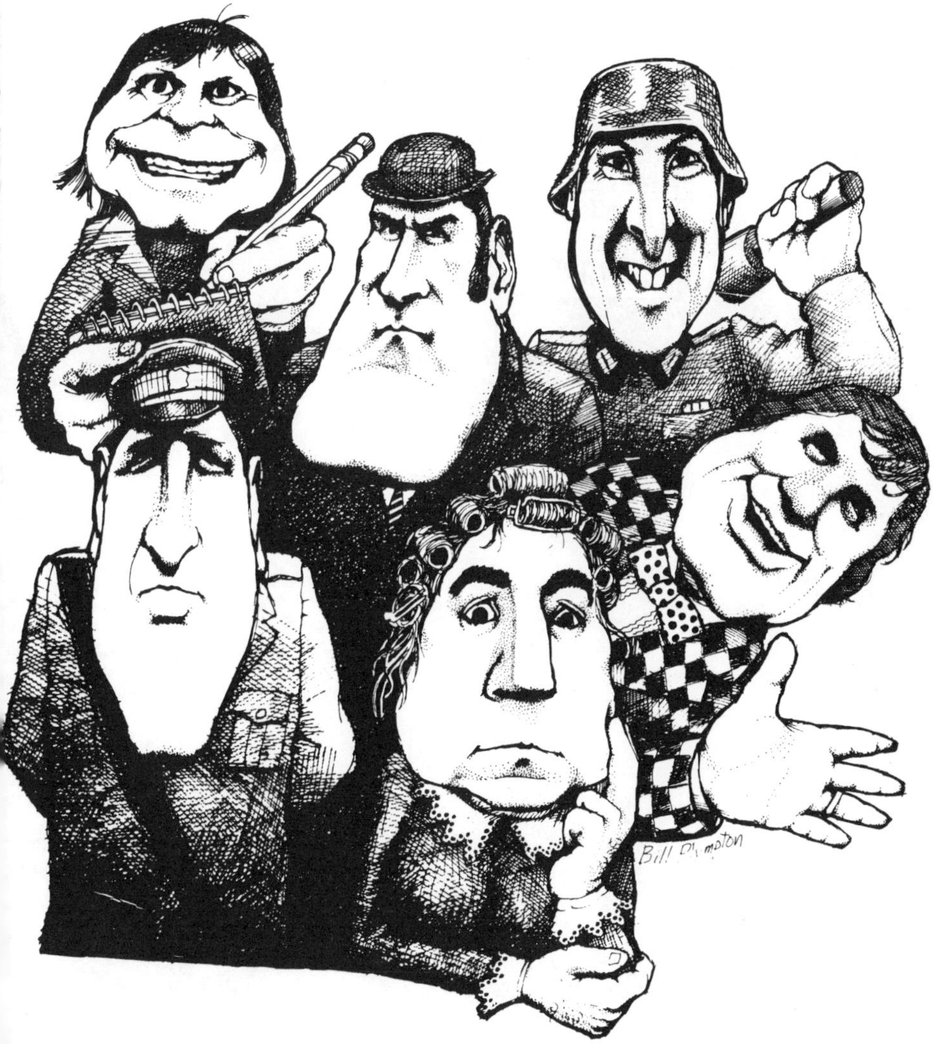

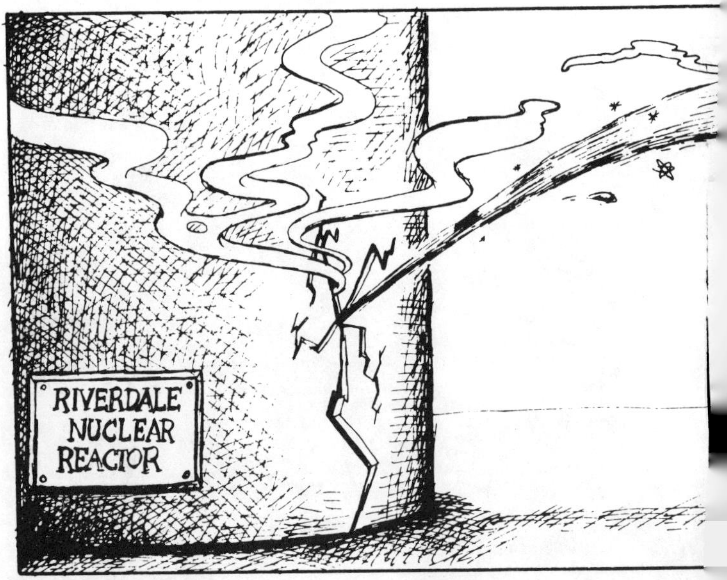
RIVERDALE NUCLEAR REACTOR

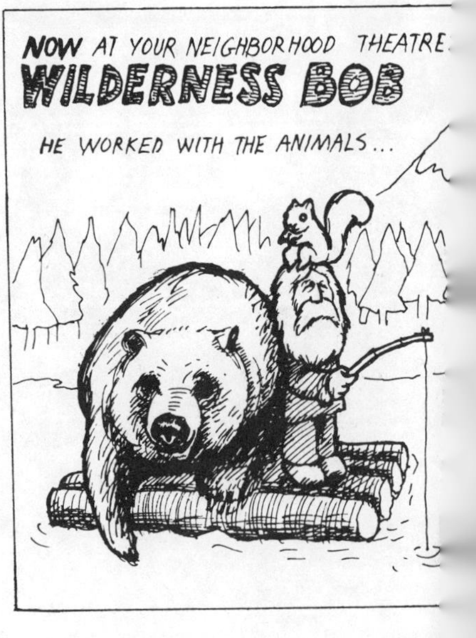
NOW AT YOUR NEIGHBORHOOD THEATRE
WILDERNESS BOB
HE WORKED WITH THE ANIMALS...

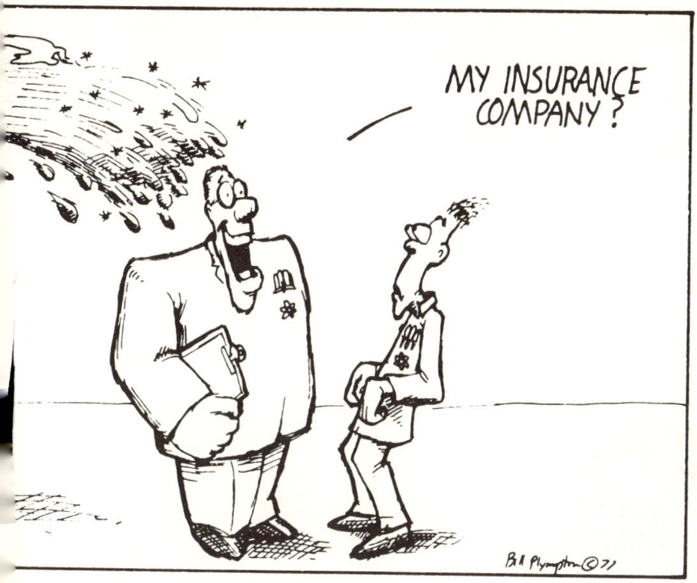
MY INSURANCE COMPANY?
Bill Plympton © 77

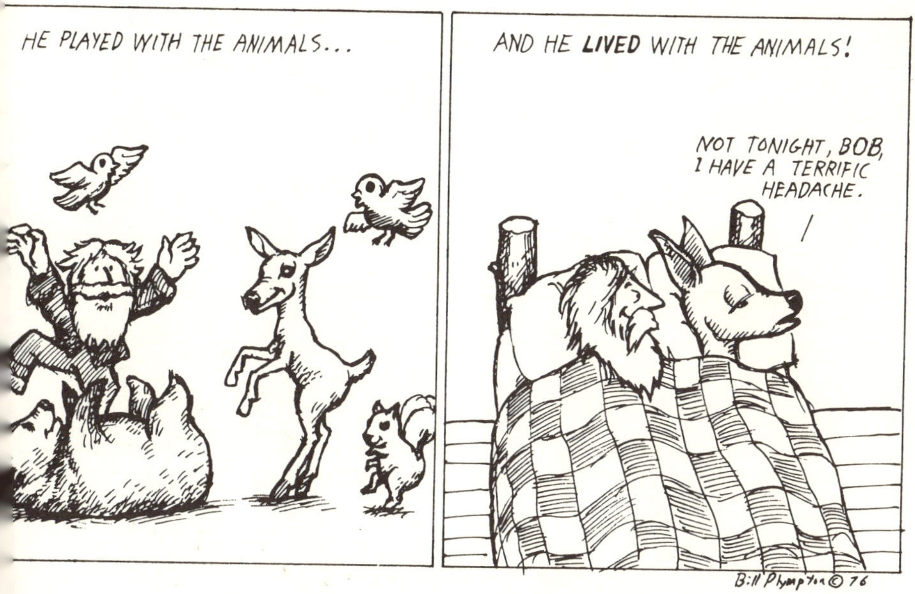
HE PLAYED WITH THE ANIMALS...
AND HE LIVED WITH THE ANIMALS!
NOT TONIGHT, BOB, I HAVE A TERRIFIC HEADACHE.
Bill Plympton © 76

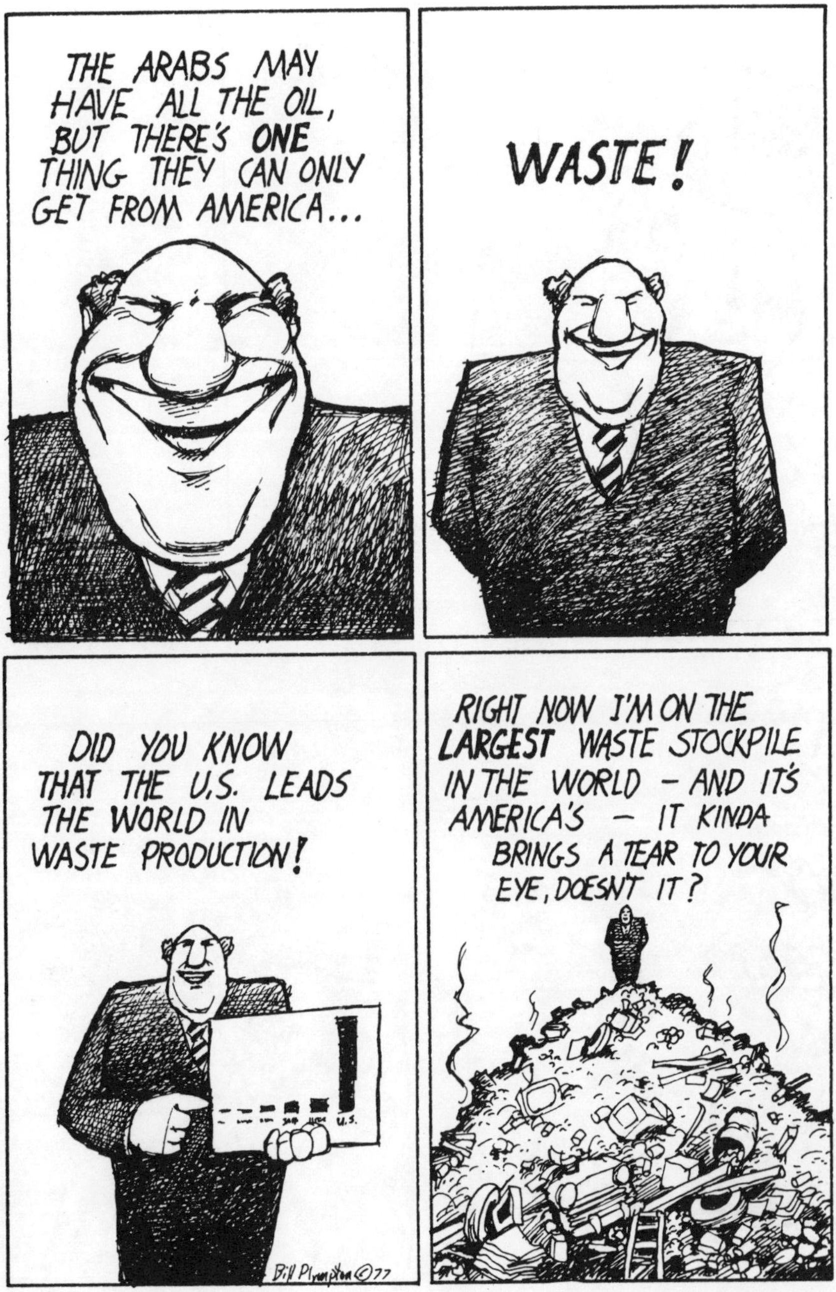
THE ARABS MAY HAVE ALL THE OIL, BUT THERE'S ONE THING THEY CAN ONLY GET FROM AMERICA...
WASTE!
DID YOU KNOW THAT THE U.S. LEADS THE WORLD IN WASTE PRODUCTION!
U.S.
Bill Plympton ©77
RIGHT NOW I'M ON THE LARGEST WASTE STOCKPILE IN THE WORLD – AND IT'S AMERICA'S – IT KINDA BRINGS A TEAR TO YOUR EYE, DOESN'T IT?

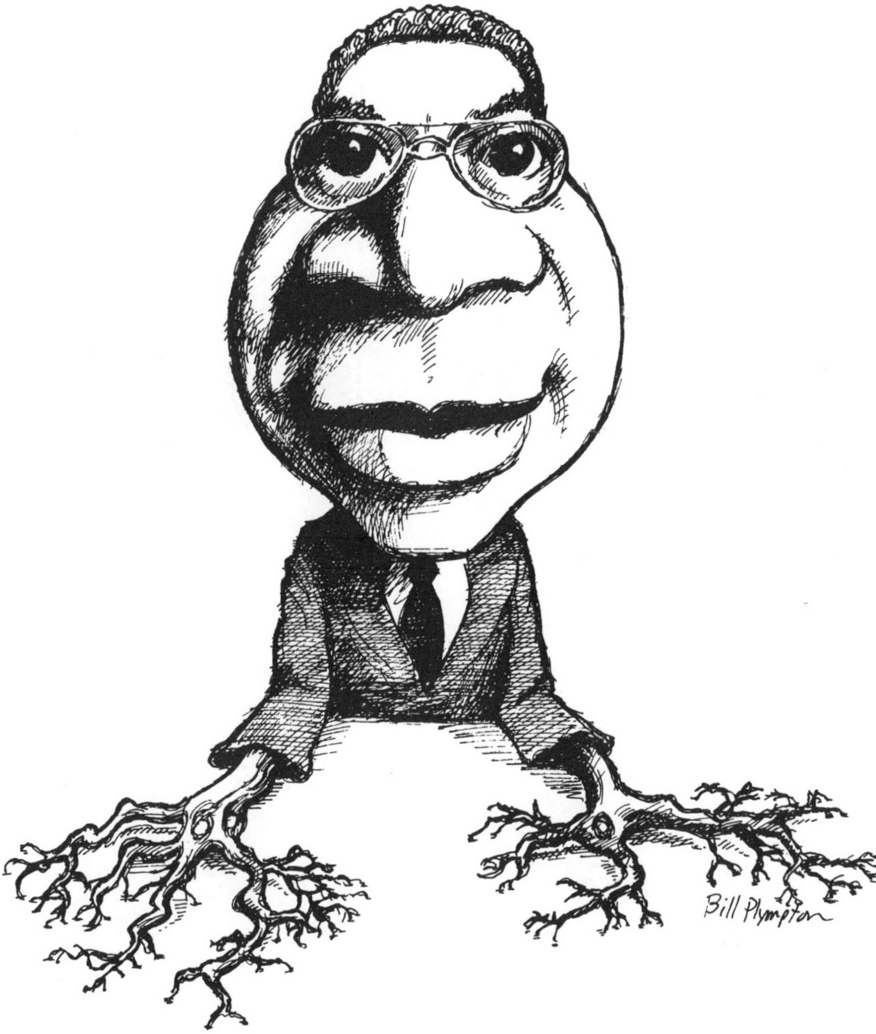
Bill Plympton

I'VE INCREASED MY EATING SPEED BY 100%! AND YOU CAN TOO... WITH EVELYN WOOD EATING DYNAMICS!
WATCH ME EAT THIS ENTIRE 7 COURSE DINNER IN 22 SECONDS!

HELLO, I'M IDI AMIN PEOPLE CRITICIZE ME FOR MY ROUGH METHODS —
BUT THEY MUST REALIZE IT'S NOT EASY BRINGING CULTURE AND MORALITY TO UGANDA.

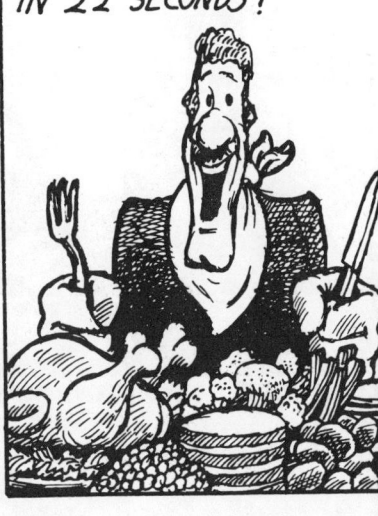

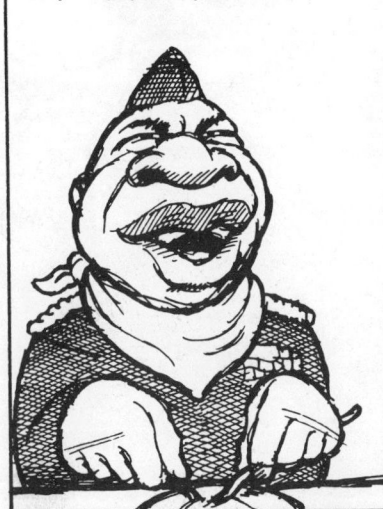

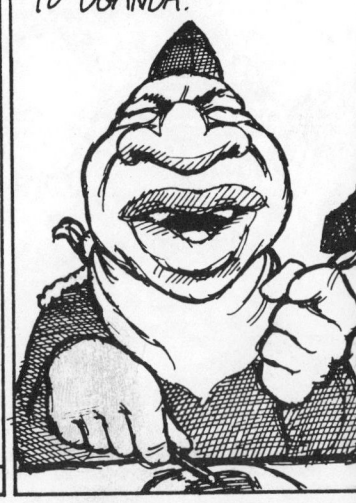

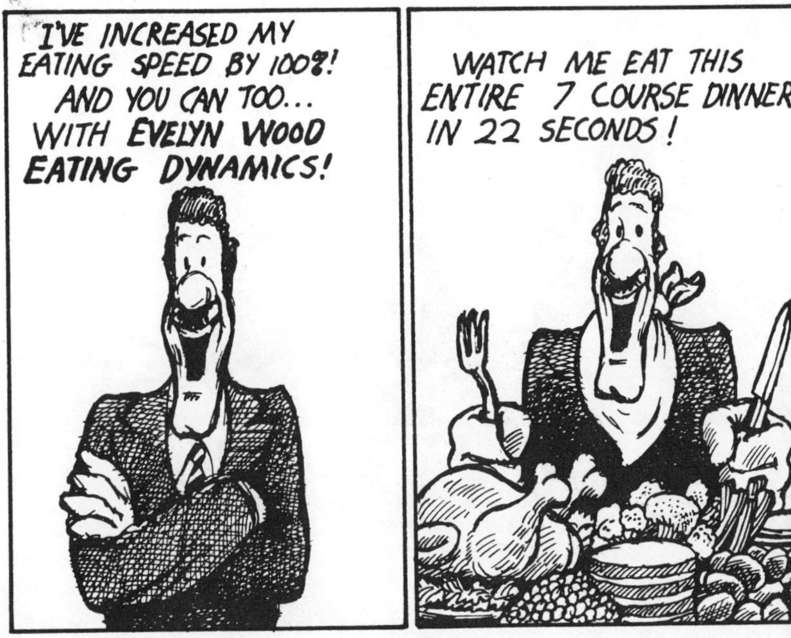

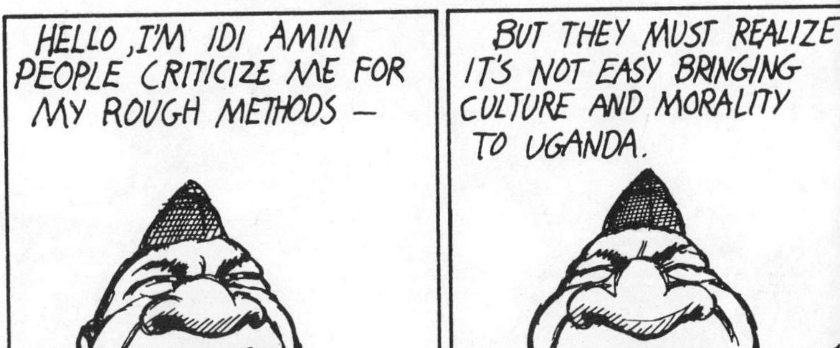

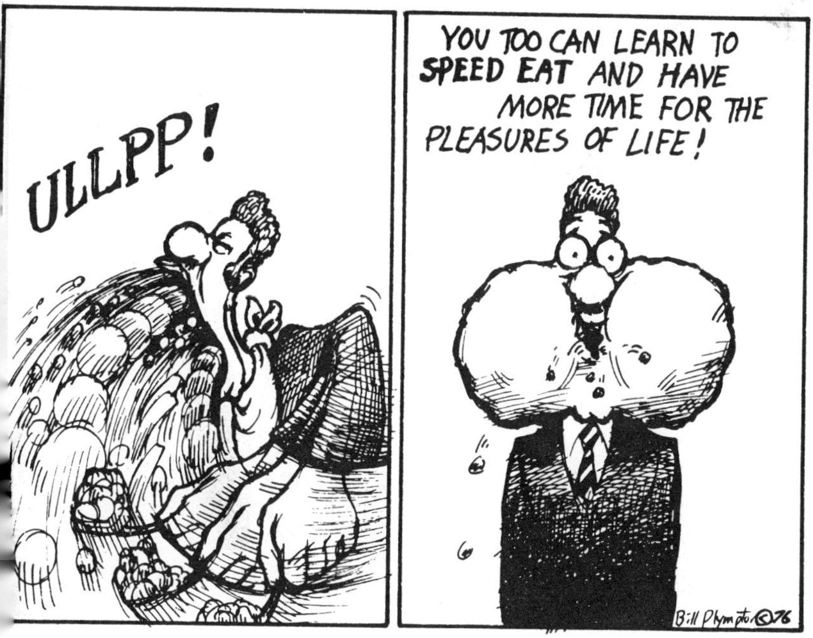
ULLPP!
YOU TOO CAN LEARN TO SPEED EAT AND HAVE MORE TIME FOR THE PLEASURES OF LIFE!
Bill Plympton ©76

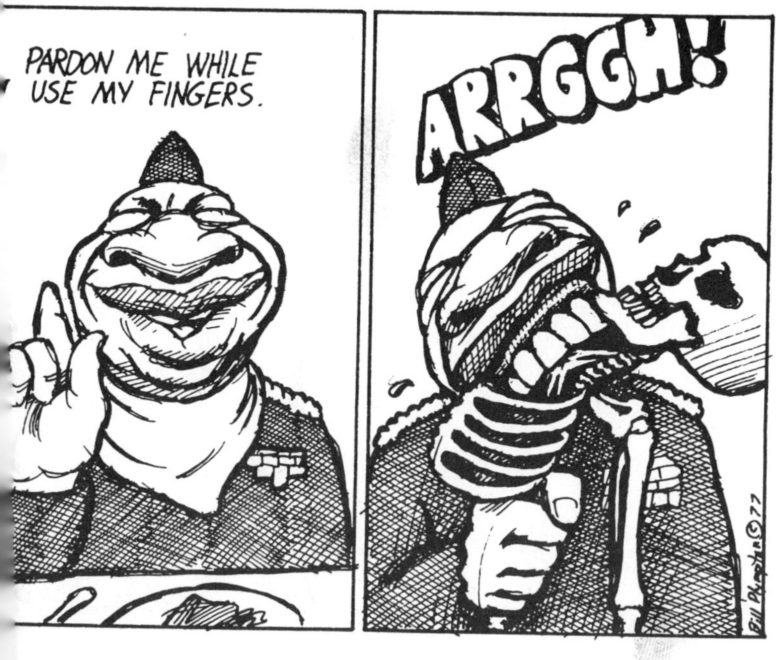
PARDON ME WHILE
USE MY FINGERS.
ARRGGH!

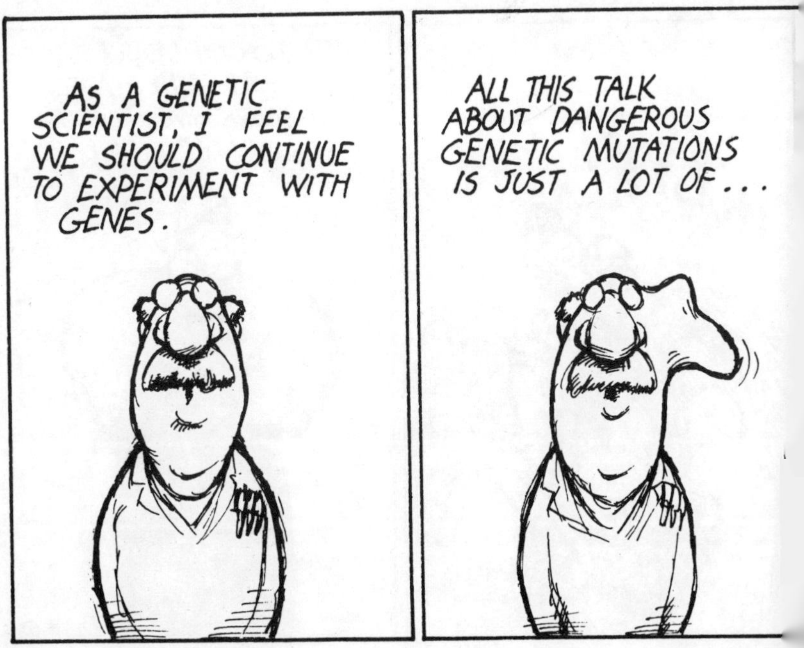
AS A GENETIC SCIENTIST, I FEEL WE SHOULD CONTINUE TO EXPERIMENT WITH GENES.
ALL THIS TALK ABOUT DANGEROUS GENETIC MUTATIONS IS JUST A LOT OF . . .

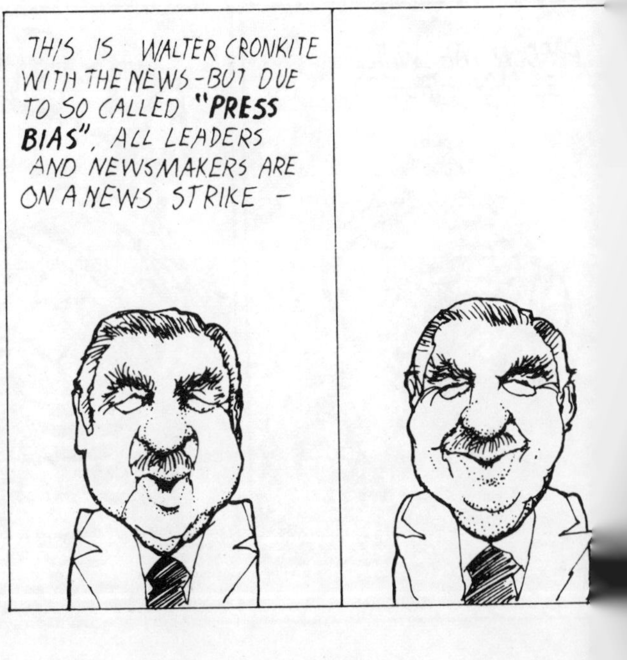
THIS IS WALTER CRONKITE WITH THE NEWS - BUT DUE TO SO CALLED "PRESS BIAS", ALL LEADERS AND NEWSMAKERS ARE ON A NEWS STRIKE -

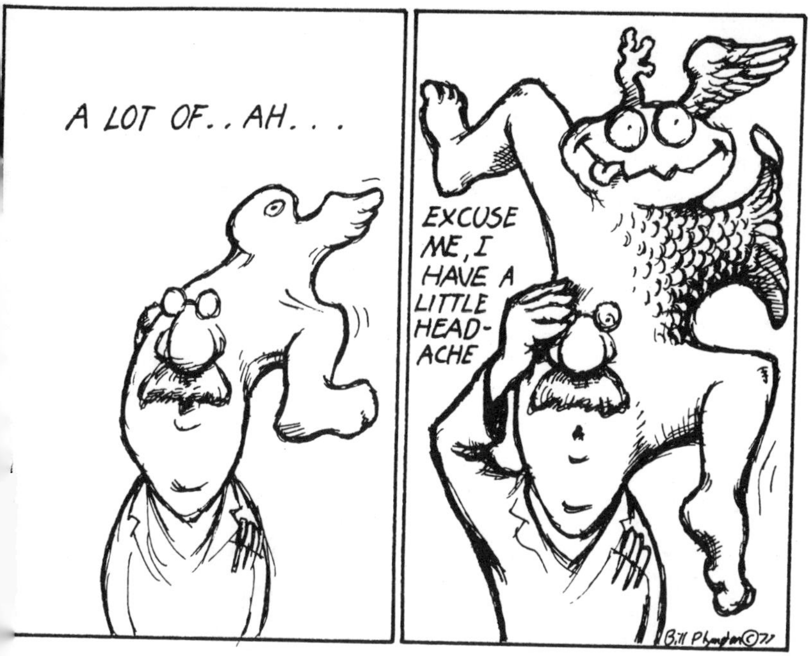
A LOT OF.. AH. . .
EXCUSE ME, I HAVE A LITTLE HEAD-ACHE
Bill Plympton©71

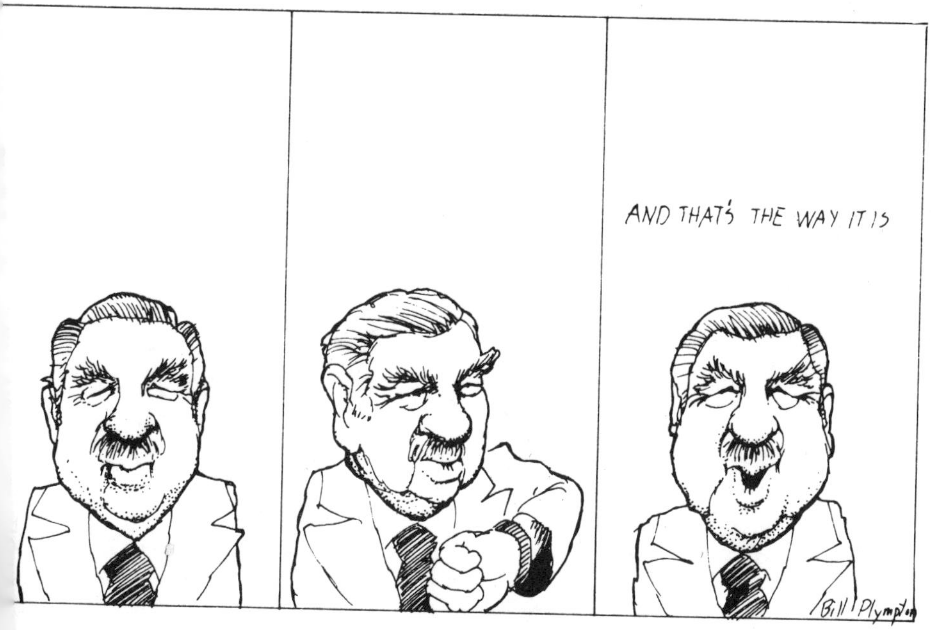
AND THAT'S THE WAY IT IS
Bill Plympton

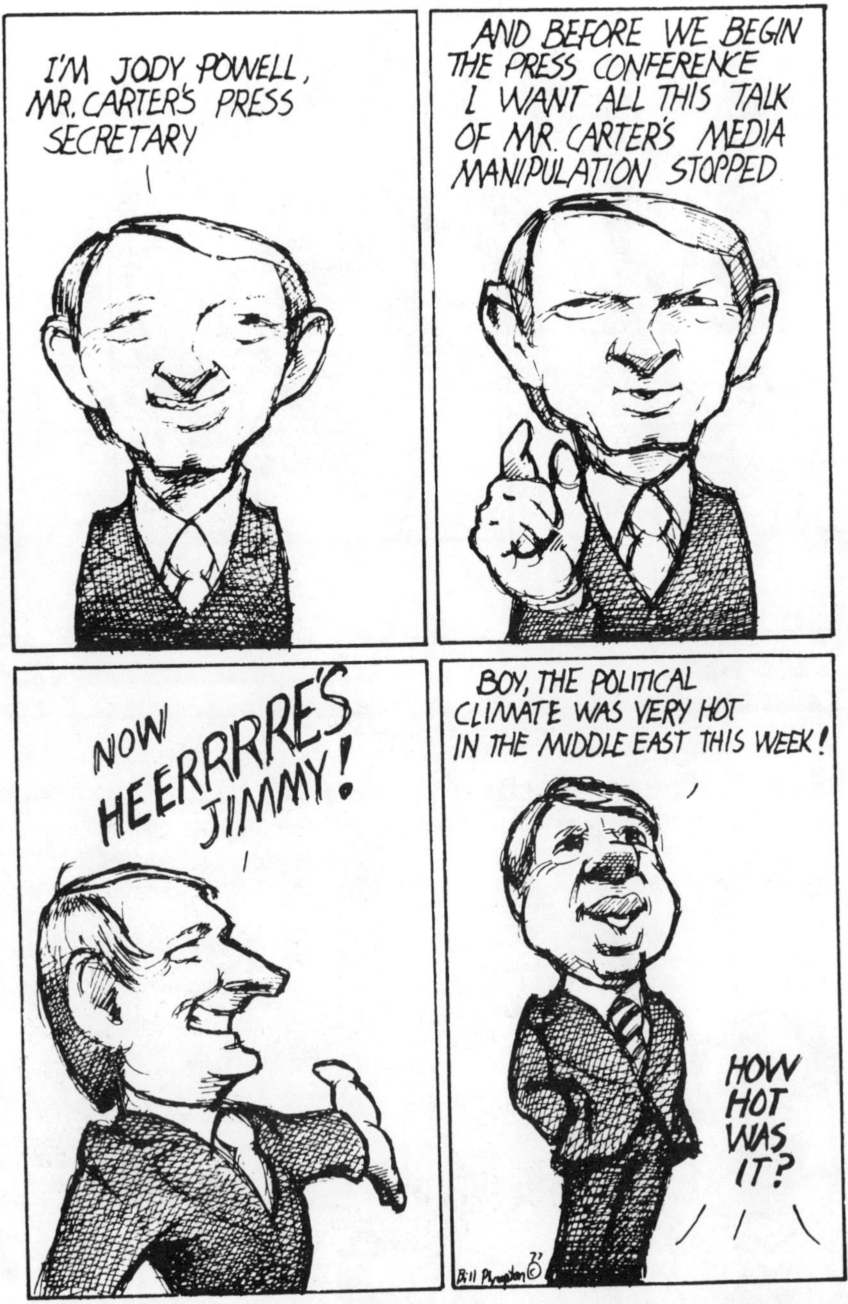
I'M JODY POWELL, MR. CARTER'S PRESS SECRETARY
AND BEFORE WE BEGIN THE PRESS CONFERENCE I WANT ALL THIS TALK OF MR. CARTER'S MEDIA MANIPULATION STOPPED
NOW HEERRRRE'S JIMMY!
BOY, THE POLITICAL CLIMATE WAS VERY HOT IN THE MIDDLE EAST THIS WEEK!
HOW HOT WAS IT?
Bill Plympton © 77

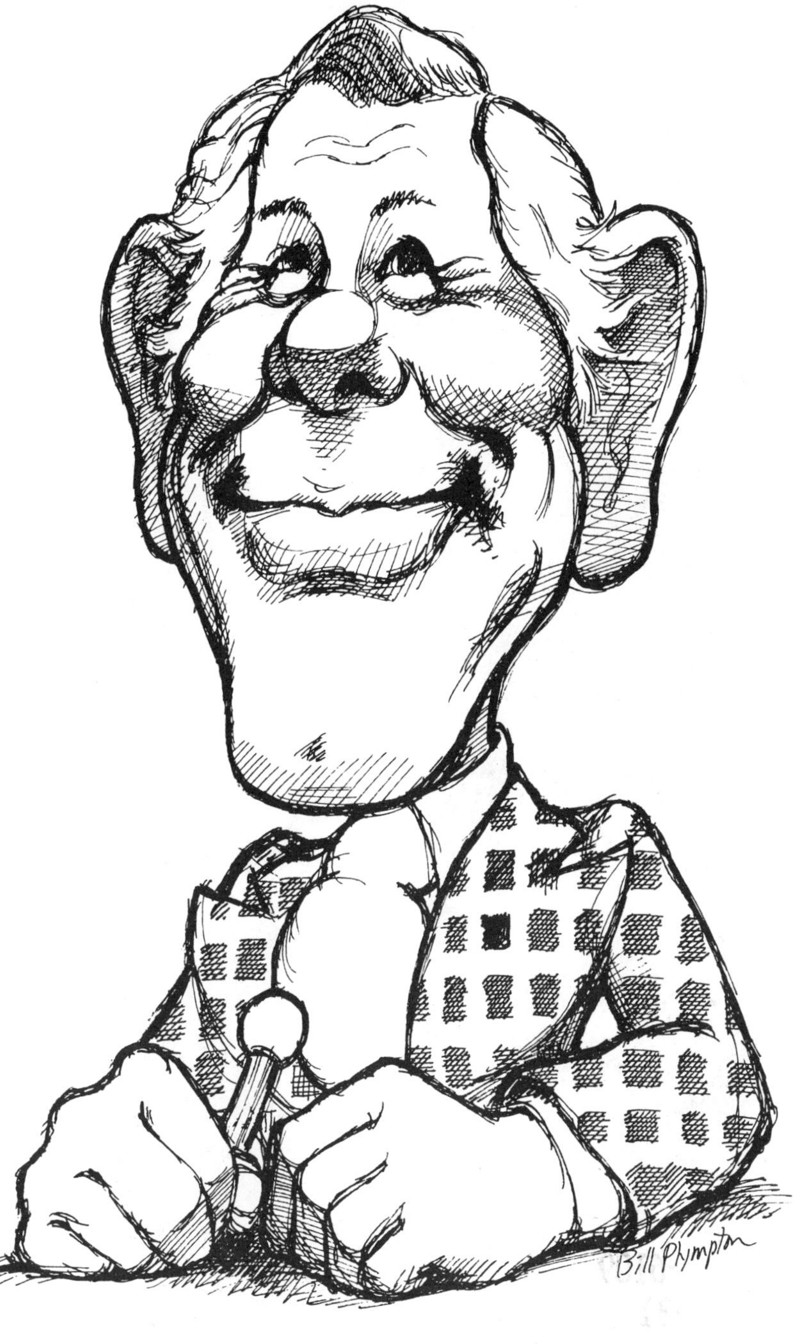
Bill Plympton

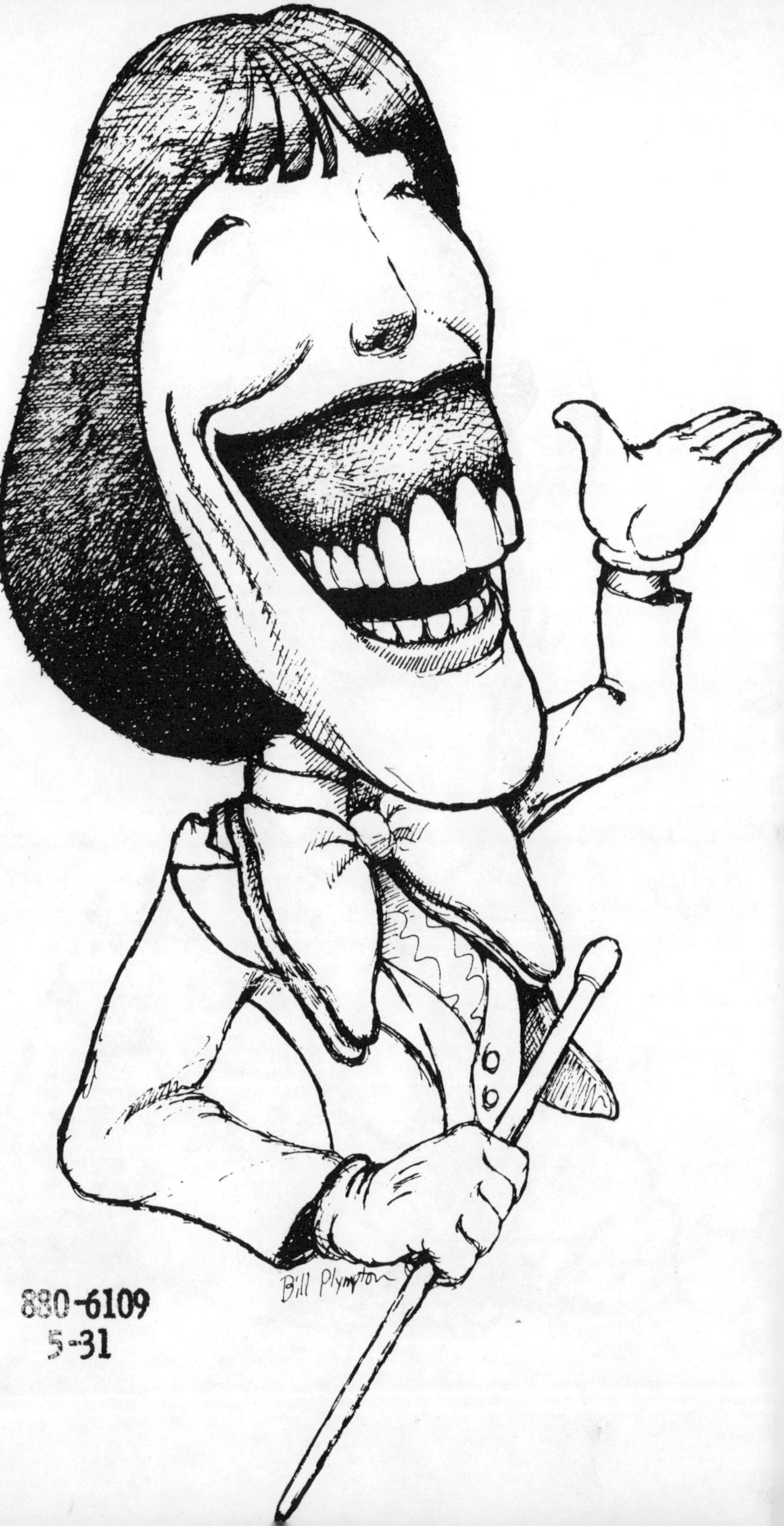
Bill Plympton

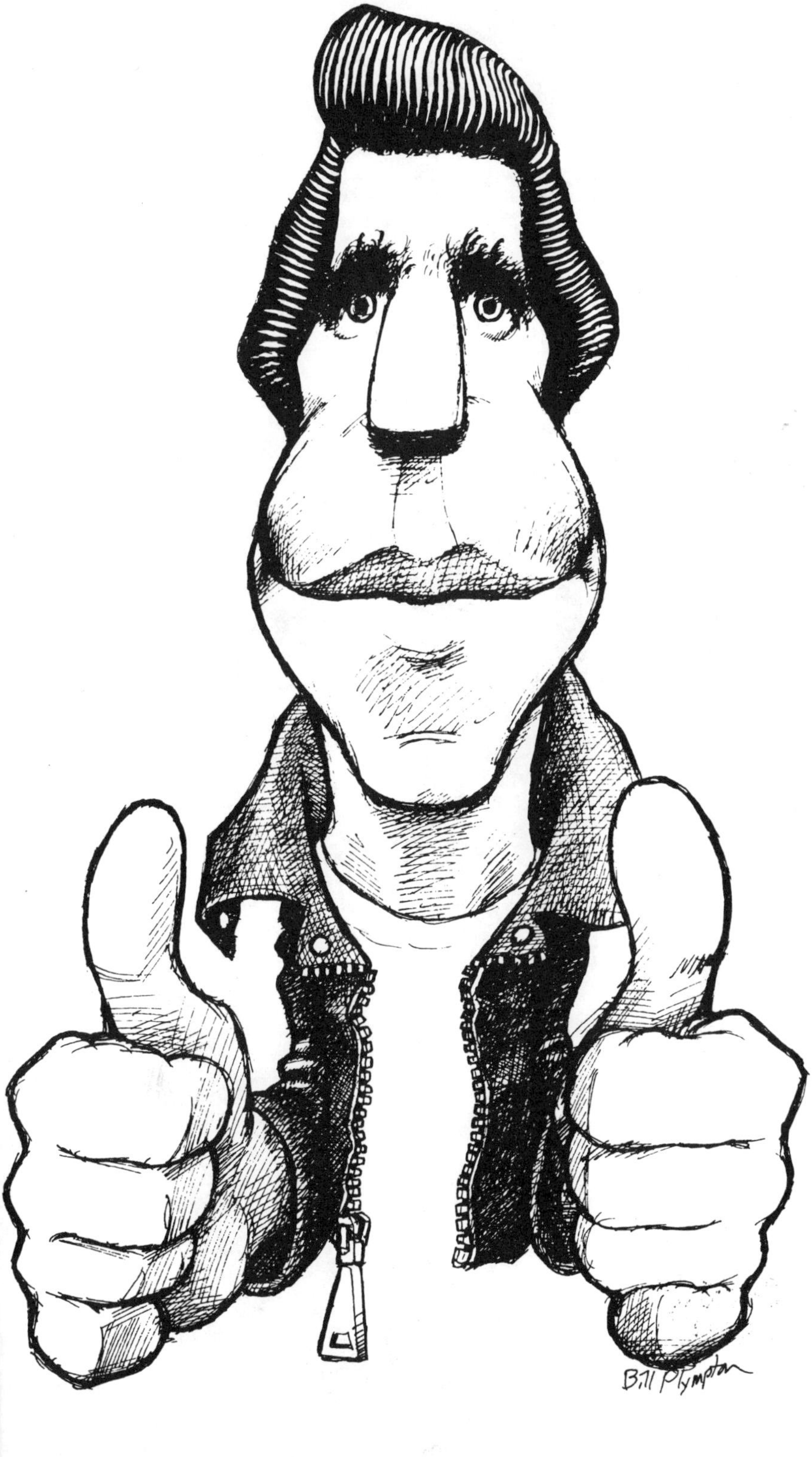
Bill Plympton

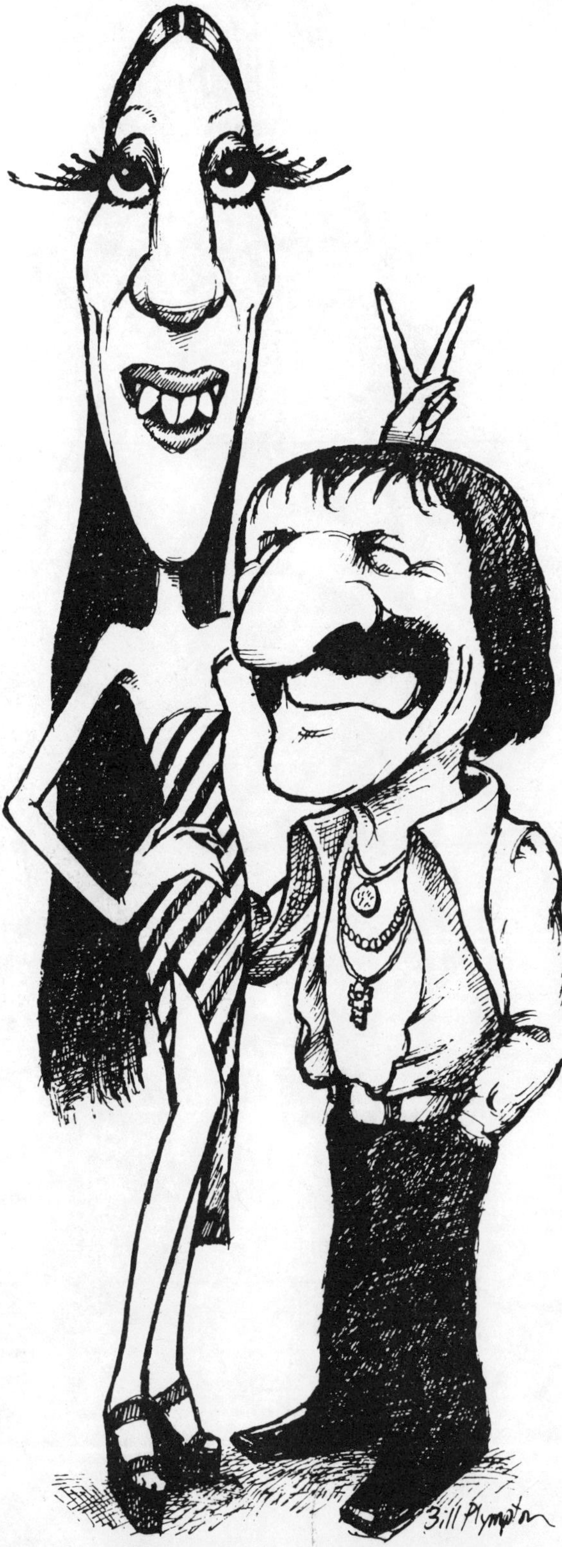
Bill Plympton

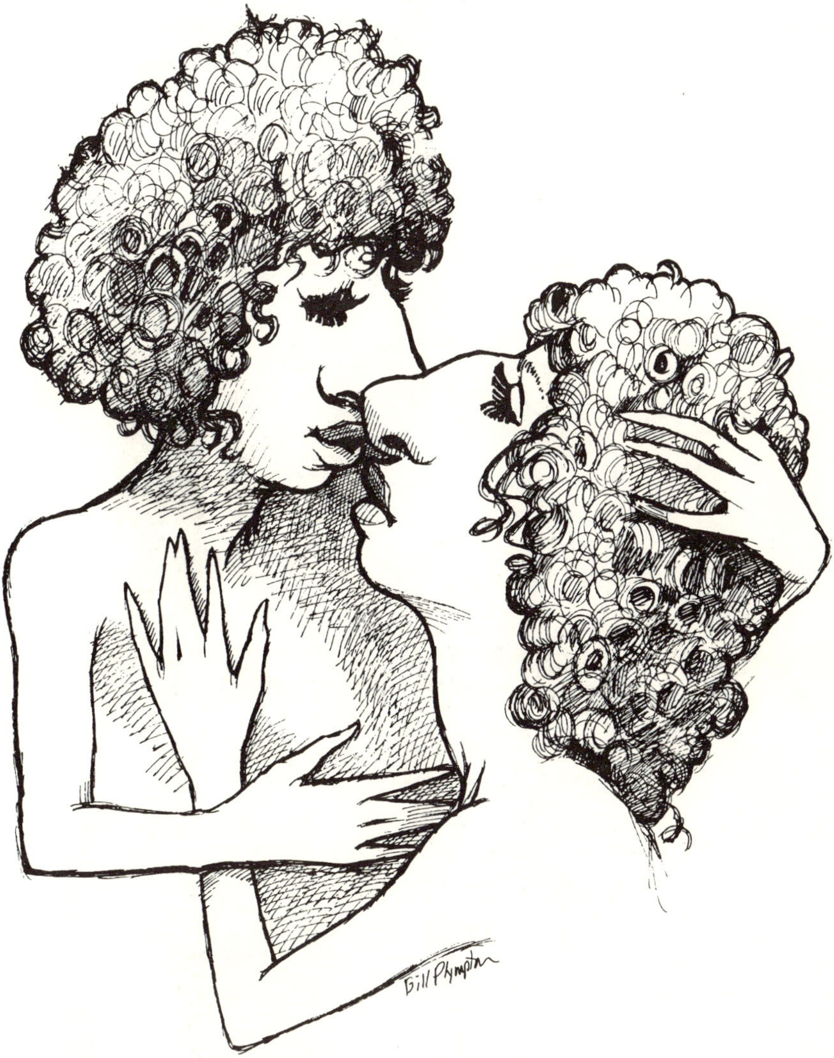
Bill Plympton

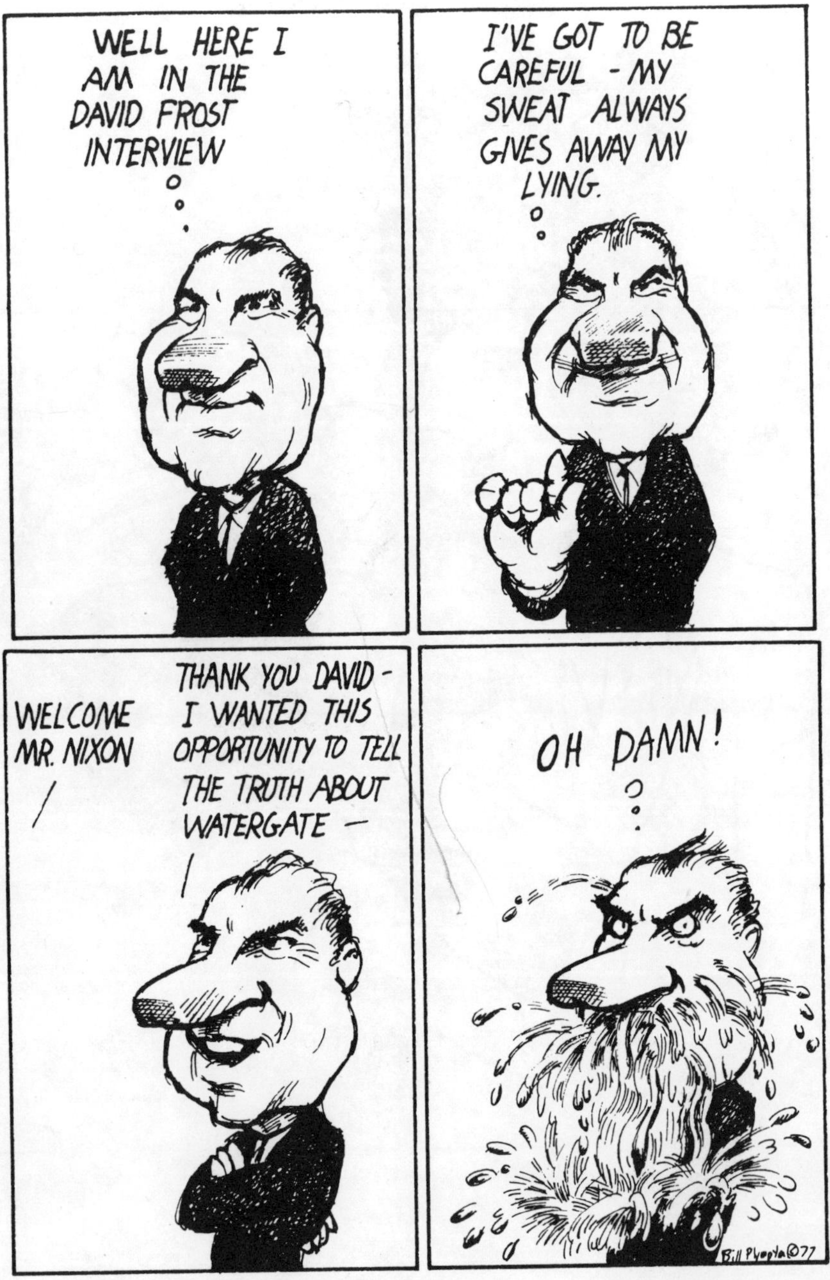
WELL HERE I AM IN THE DAVID FROST INTERVIEW
I'VE GOT TO BE CAREFUL - MY SWEAT ALWAYS GIVES AWAY MY LYING.
WELCOME MR. NIXON
THANK YOU DAVID - I WANTED THIS OPPORTUNITY TO TELL THE TRUTH ABOUT WATERGATE -
OH DAMN!
Bill Plympton ©77

Caricatures (in order of appearance)

George Plimpton
Nelson Rockefeller
Henry Kissinger
Timothy Leary
Bob Dylan
Mick Jagger
John Denver
David Brinkley
Walter Cronkite
William Buckley
Yasir Arafat
Patricia Hearst
Howard Cosell
Muhammad Ali
Mary Tyler Moore
Dolly Parton
Louise Lasser (as Mary Hartman)
Farrah Fawcett-Majors
Jimmy Carter
James Schlesinger
Johnny Cash
Peter Falk (as Colombo)
Woody Allen
Jack Nicholson
Chuck Barris ("The Gong Show")
Monty Python
Alex Haley
Johnny Carson
Lily Tomlin
Henry Winkler (as "the Fonz")
Sonny and Cher
Barbra Streisand and friend